KIDNAPPED

AT CHRISTMAS

A PLAY BY WILLIS HALL

Samuel French

and

Heinemann Educational Books

First published 1975
Reprinted 1976, 1979, 1980, 1983,
1986, 1987, 1990

Published jointly by Samuel French Ltd
26 Southampton Street London WC2E 7JE

New York Toronto Sydney Hollywood

and by

Heinemann Educational Books Ltd
Halley Court, Jordan Hill, Oxford OX2 8EJ
OXFORD LONDON EDINBURGH
MELBOURNE SYDNEY AUCKLAND
IBADAN NAIROBI GABORONE HARARE
KINGSTON PORTSMOUTH NH (USA)
SINGAPORE MADRID

ISBN (Samuel French) 0 573 05037 6
ISBN (Heinemann) 0 435 23368 8

Printed and bound in Great Britain by
Richard Clay Ltd, Bungay, Suffolk

CHARACTERS: Convict Gilbert
Convict Crosby
Warder Mullins
Warder MacBain
Detective Constable Grummett
Clara Grummett (his wife)
Alexander Grummett (their son)
Evadne Docherty
Headmaster Horace Winston Allardyce

SETTINGS: A prison cell
Outside the prison wall
The Grummetts' living room
A police station
Another wall
A spooky green cellar

ACT ONE
Scene One

Two men, Gilbert and Crosby, are spending Christmas in prison. Gilbert is sitting on a chair, reading a comic. Crosby is lying on his top bunk bed, restless.

Gilbert   *(singing)* Good King Wenceslas knocked a bobby senseless, right in the middle of Marks and Spencers . . .

Crosby   *Shut up!*

Gilbert   Sorry. *(Pause)* Good King Wenceslas looked out, of his bedroom winder, when a poor man came in sight, he gave him a red-hot cinder . . .

Crosby   *Shut up!*

Gilbert   I'm only trying to cheer us up, Crosby.

Crosby   Don't bother. *(Getting up)* This is no place to be at Christmas, this is no place to be at all! Shall I tell you something, Gilbert? This is the worst possible place to be on Christmas Eve, bar none.

Gilbert   Shall I sing, While shepherds watched their turnip tops?

Crosby   No! You know where we should be tonight, don't you? Out there—doing evil things. Sawing down the Christmas Tree in Trafalgar Square; chucking a brick through a toy-shop window; mugging carol singers. All like that. This could be the best night of the year for us, and where are we? In flippin' clink.

Gilbert   Chicken dinner tomorrow, Crosby, and Christmas pud.

Crosby   Chicken dinner? Chicken dinner? I don't want no chicken dinner. Not *prison* chicken dinner, all cold and greasy; horrible clammy sprouts, lumpy mashed spuds, greasy gravy. I want my freedom, matey, that's what I want. I want to enjoy myself. What prison are we in?

Gilbert   Maximum security.

Crosby   I thought we must be. I thought they'd put us in with a load of rascals and villains. *(Gazing at the audience)* Look at 'em! Did you ever see such a collection of rogues and vagabonds? Fancy being stuck here over Christmas with all them ugly-mugs staring at you.

Gilbert   *(studies the audience, then)* The little ones aren't too bad, Crosby, it's the big ones that are ugly. Some of the little ones don't look all that bad at all.

Crosby	They all look horrible. Horrible. I'll tell you, matey, I've been in a lot of nicks: Dartmoor, the Ville, Wormwood Scrubs, but I've never before been locked up with a bunch as ugly as this lot here. Never. And it's fizzin' Christmas Eve, would you believe? What are this lot in for? Frightening babies?
Gilbert	They're the audience.
Crosby	They're still horrible.
Gilbert	Mums and dads and kids. They could help us to escape.
Crosby	Escape?
Gilbert	Yes.
Crosby	Tonight?
Gilbert	Yes.
Crosby	Do you think they would?
Gilbert	I don't know. If you stop calling them names they might. If you could try and be a bit more *nice* to them.

> *Crosby thinks it over, then adopts an ingratiating smile.*

Crosby	Hello, Kiddies! Hello, little children! Hello mums and dads! Are you all enjoying yourselves—I hope so. 'Cos if you're not enjoying yourselves, I'll break out of here, be in them stalls like a dose of salts, and I'll duff up the lot of you!
Gilbert	Is that the nicest you can be?
Crosby	Not nice enough?
Gilbert	Nowhere near. They're hardly likely to help us, are they, if you talk to them like that.
Crosby	I'll try again. Hello, Kiddiewinkies! Are all the good children sitting comfortably? Who's going to help their nice kind Uncle Crosby get out of the nasty cruel prison then? Did I hear somebody say 'not me'? Did one of you horrible monsters say 'not me'? My life, I'll be over the end of that stage and clipping earholes faster than you can say hard labour!

> *Remembering himself, he glances guiltily at Gilbert who shakes his head.*

Crosby	Let me have another try. Let's find out how many of these lovely boys and girls are going to help us to escape. All the ones who are going to help us get out of this prison, raise your right hands. High up in the air. Now, all the ones who want us to stay locked up,

raise your left hands. Right—all the ones with their
right hands in the air, turn round and duff up all of
them with their left hands up.

Gilbert   No, no, no, no! That's no good either.

Crosby   I've got another one. Hands up all the little boys and
girls who came in daddy's car this afternoon? Mummy's
car? If you came on the bus or the tube, stick your
hands in your pockets and keep shtum. Only those
who came in a motor-car with daddy or mummy put
their hands up. Good. Now I want you to slip your
hand, nicely and gently, into daddy's pocket or
mummy's handbag and nick the car keys.

Gilbert   That's worse than ever.

Crosby   I don't see why. If we're going to make a quick
getaway we're going to need some wheels.

Gilbert   I've got a better idea. Can you all shout out loud?
Can you shout, 'Your shoe-lace is undone'? Again.
And every time I scratch my nose, I want to hear you
shout, 'Your shoe-lace is undone'. Shall we try it?
(He scratches his nose) Again. *(He scratches his nose
again)* Very good.

Crosby   Aren't you going to fasten it?

Gilbert   Fasten what?

Crosby	Your shoe-lace?
Gilbert	What shoe-lace?
Crosby	The one that's undone.
Gilbert	It isn't undone.
Crosby	It isn't mine is it?
Gilbert	Nobody's shoe-lace is undone. It's all part of the plan. To escape. With their help. Listen to this, and tell me what you think. I create a fuss—we both kick up a fuss. We start shouting and screaming until the warder comes. He says, 'Why are you kicking up a fuss?' He says, 'What are you shouting and screaming about?' We say, 'Help us, save us, save us! There's a big hairy spider climbing up the wall . . .'
Crosby	Where? Where is it? I'll smash it! I'll stamp on it! I'll spifflicate it! I hate spiders—horrible hairy things!
Gilbert	There isn't really a spider. That's just what we tell him. We make the spider up. The warder comes into our cell. He gets out his truncheon to bash the spider with. I scratch my nose. Like this. They shout, 'Your shoe-lace is undone'. The warder gives you his truncheon to hold while he bends down to tie up his shoe. Then, while he's bending down, you bop him on the nut.
Crosby	With his truncheon.
Gilbert	Yes.
Crosby	Great, Gilbert!
Gilbert	Do you really like it?
Crosby	Fantastic. I hate warders. I hate warders more than anything. I'll give it to him, wham-bam, right on his head. Great.
Gilbert	Not too hard though.
Crosby	Just hard enough.
Gilbert	Off we go then.

The pair of them start to scream and shout and generally kick up a fuss. Warder Mullins enters.

Mullins	Orlright, orlright—knock it off. There's quite a number of respectable convicts in here trying to get some sleep.
Gilbert } Crosby }	Help! Help! Save us! Save us!
Mullins	What's it all in aid of anyway? Why are you kicking up a fuss? What's all this shouting and screaming about?

Gilbert } Crosby }	Oh, help us, Warder Mullins! Save us! There's a great big hairy spider climbing up the wall of our cell!
Mullins	Are you sure?
Gilbert	Its legs are that long!
Crosby	It's all hairy and horrible, Warder Mullins!
Mullins	Let's have a look.

> *The warder produces an impressive key, unlocks the door, and enters the cell. He produces his truncheon.*

Mullins	Whereabouts is it?
Gilbert	Over there.

> *Gilbert scratches his nose, but when the audience call out, 'Your shoe-lace is undone', it is Crosby who bends down to investigate his footwear.*

Mullins	Come on—where is it?

> *Gilbert behind the warder's back, makes elaborate gestures at Crosby who gets the message.*

Gilbert	Hang on, Warder, I've lost it now—I'll look again.

> *Gilbert scratches his nose again. The audience call out again. Crosby waits gleefully for the warder to react, but again the warder doesn't move. The ritual is gone through yet again.*

Mullins	Well? Where's this horrible hairy spider? I'm still waiting, both of you! If this is your idea of a joke . . .
Gilbert	Excuse me, Warder, but I think your shoe-lace is undone.
Crosby	I'll hold your truncheon for you, if you like while you tie it up again.
Mullins	*(without looking down)* Not my shoe-lace. I never use them. I wear special-issue prison-officer heavy-duty elastic-sided boots. Now then, where's this horrible hairy spider?
Gilbert	I can't see it now. It must have gone away, Mr Mullins.

> *But as Gilbert is speaking, a horrible hairy spider descends from above, unnoticed by Gilbert and Crosby. The enormous spider terrifies the Warder who quakes in his elastic-sided boots, and then bolts, slamming the cell door behind him. The spider disappears again.*

Crosby	It didn't work, did it?
Gilbert	Not quite.
Crosby	We'll be stuck in here all over Christmas. For prison chicken dinner and it'll be all slimy and greasy, with clammy sprouts, lumpy spuds and greasy gravy.
Gilbert	Perhaps it won't be all that bad.
Crosby	It'll be horrible. No crackers—they don't have crackers. I hate not having crackers. I'll probably end up throwing clammy sprouts at one of the warders, then they'll put me into solitary confinement. I'll tell you something else as well.
Gilbert	What's that?
Crosby	My shoe-lace *is* undone.
Gilbert	What do you want me to do about it?
Crosby	I was wondering if you would tie it up for me? I can't do double-bows. I *hate* double-bows. I can do single bows but they're always coming loose. And if I tie knots I can never undo them.
Gilbert	Give us your foot.

> *As Gilbert is tying Crosby's shoe, the horrible hairy spider descends again. Gilbert sees it first, and reacts with horror. Crosby follows his glance. They dash for the cell door—and find it unlocked. Once they are out on the other side, they react with surprise.*

Crosby	We're out!
Gilbert	He forgot to lock it!
Crosby	We're free!
Gilbert	Very nearly. Come on, let's make a dash for it.

> *But as they cross the stage, the Warder returns with Warder MacBain. The Warders carry guns and have come in pursuit of the spider, which has vanished again. Crosby and Gilbert duck into the shadows as the two Warders approach the empty cell, cautiously. The Warders peer up towards the ceiling.*

MacBain	Are you sure you're not having me on, Mr Mullins?
Mullins	Have I ever lied to you, Mr MacBain?
MacBain	No, but you have been known to exaggerate slightly.
Mullins	Not this time—it was enormous. *And* horrible *and* hairy.

MacBain   You're sure you haven't been treating yourself to an
           unofficial glassful of the Governor's Christmas Day
           medium-dry sherry?

Mullins   All right then—don't believe me. Don't take my word for
           it. I wasn't the only one that saw the spider. Gilbert and
           Crosby saw it first--they shouted for me to come and
           look at it. *(He looks down at the lower half of the cell
           and is immediately suspicious)* Hang on! Hold up!

MacBain   What is it now—I suppose you've seen a six foot cockroach?

Mullins   Not at all. Do me a favour, would you? Check the
           contents of this cell. Just go over the inventory in your
           head and tell me if you notice anything untoward or
           missing?

MacBain   No—not on a cursory inspection. Two beds, convicts for
           the use of, two chairs, similar, one table, two little
           enamelled potties . . . Wait a minute, now that you come
           to mention it—there's two convicts missing!

                      *Warder Mullins tries the cell door and finds it
                      unlocked.*

Mullins   They've done a bunk! Convicts Gilbert and Crosby have
           hopped it!

                      *At which point, Gilbert and Crosby break from
                      cover in the shadows and seek refuge in the
                      audience. The two Warders produce whistles,
                      blow short sharp blasts, and pursue the convicts
                      in a wild chase around the auditorium. At the
                      end of the chase we have lost both the convicts
                      and the warders.*

                      *A Detective, Grummett, enters and addresses
                      the audience.*

Grummett   Right then—nobody move! My name is Detective
           Constable Stephen Grummett, C.I.D., and it is my duty

to tell you that nobody will be allowed to leave this auditorium, not even to get a tub of chocolate ice-cream or to go to the lavvy. Two convicts, Crosby and Gilbert, have made their escape from off this stage and it's believed that the breakout took place with the assistance of a person or persons unknown, most probably a member or members of this audience. During the next two hours, I shall pass among you all taking the names and addresses of every man, woman, boy and girl sitting out there. In order not to cause you too much inconvenience, it has been decided to allow the play to continue up here, while I'm out there. And I look forward to receiving the maximum co-operation from you all. The sooner we get everything cleared up, the sooner we can all go home. I shall be commencing my enquiries about there—*(He waves towards the back of the Stalls)*—somewhere. I do have my eye on a particularly suspicious-looking male parent in Row 'M'. Yes, sir, you, sir, you know who I mean. The gentleman in the brown suit with the glass and the bag of liquorice all-sorts. I'm on my way to join you—and it's to be hoped that the child that is with you can offer a reasonable explanation for your being here.

The Detective goes off.

Scene Two

Outside the Prison wall. A knotted sheet comes over the wall and Crosby and Gilbert climb down, clumsily, and drop to the ground, one on top of the other. They clamber to their feet.

Gilbert   We're out! We've really made it, Crosby! Oh, *great*! Now we are free!

Crosby examines himself, gingerly.

Gilbert   Are you all right?

Crosby   I think you've trodden on my ear. Does it look as if it's swelling up to you?

Gilbert   I can't see anything. Never mind your ear—we're out in the open air at last, man! After all that time behind those iron bars—we're free—and it's Christmas Eve—isn't it a terrific feeling?

Crosby	I'm not sure. I think I felt a speck of rain.
Gilbert	So? Never mind a speck of rain—a drop of rain never hurt nobody.
Crosby	I hate rain, Gilbert. I do, I really hate it. Whenever I'm out in the rain, I seem to get wetter than other people. I think the rain has got it in for me.
Gilbert	It was only a speck. It might go away. Rain, rain go away —come again on visiting day! We're free! What about all those evil things you wanted to do? All those things you were looking forward to?
Crosby	What things?
Gilbert	Robbing carol-singers you said, for one thing.
Crosby	I shouldn't think there'll be any carol-singers about to rob, not if it's pouring down with rain.
Gilbert	Chucking a brick through the toy-shop window.
Crosby	Where am I going to get a brick at this time of night?
Gilbert	We'll *look* for a brick. If it'll make you happy. Or what about going to Trafalgar Square and sawing down the Christmas Tree?
Crosby	I haven't got a saw.
Gilbert	We'll *steal* a saw. Anything for a quiet life.
Crosby	It won't be much fun though, will it? Standing in the pouring rain, soaked through to the skin, freezing to death, shivering, with a swollen ear and a rusty saw, hacking away at a dripping Christmas Tree.
Gilbert	Cheer up, Crosby—we'll find some shelter if it starts to rain.
Crosby	Where?
Gilbert	Anywhere. We'll break in somewhere. We'll climb through somebody's window. I know—we'll climb through the window of a big posh house. We're supposed to be desperate criminals, aren't we? Come on.

Crosby looks back longingly at the wall.

Crosby	I'm not at all sure we weren't better off in there.
Gilbert	It was you that wanted to escape in the first place.
Crosby	We can all make mistakes, you know. It's not too late to break back into our cell again.
Gilbert	What for?
Crosby	At least we knew where our next meal was coming from in there.

Gilbert   Yes, and what kind of a meal was it going to be?
             Clammy sprouts, lumpy spuds and greasy gravy.

Crosby   It's better than clammy, lumpy, greasy nothing.

Gilbert   Come *on*, Crosby. Keep your chin up. We'll commit
             a robbery.

                      *But before they can set off, Detective
                      Constable Grummett enters through the
                      Auditorium.*

             Quick! Hide!

                      *Grummett walks up onto the stage, does not
                      see Gilbert and Crosby, and addresses the
                      audience.*

Grummett   Right then—so far so good. *(He displays his notebook)*
             I've made a fair start. I have already written down the
             names and addresses and particulars of twenty
             eye-witnesses and interviewed a number of likely
             suspects. I have also made a special note of one very
             cheeky boy, Freddie Hardacre, aged nine. And when
             he next returns to school, he'll no doubt find himself
             reporting to his headmaster. Let that act as a warning
             to the more high-spirited ones among you. *(A movement
             in the shadows causes him to turn)* Who's there? There's
             somebody there. Come out, with your hands up high,
             or else I'll shoot!

                      *Gilbert and Crosby emerge with their hands
                      above their heads.*

Gilbert   Don't shoot Detective Constable Grummett, it's only us!

Grummett   Convicts Gilbert and Crosby—I knew you wouldn't be
             on the loose for long.

Crosby   I hate you, Grummett—I do, I really hate you.

Grummett   No fishy business mind—get those hands up higher. This
             isn't a toy gun I'm holding, you know.

                      *During the following exchange, Crosby and
                      Gilbert keep their hands up.*

Gilbert   It isn't any kind of gun, Detective Constable Grummett.
             It's your whistle.

Grummett   Is it? Well, I'm blowed.

Gilbert   So's your whistle.

Grummett   I beg your pardon?

Gilbert   It's a joke, Detective Constable Grummett. Your
             whistle—blowed—don't you get it?

Crosby   *I* don't get it, Gilbert.

Grummett   Hey, hey, hey! I didn't say anything about taking your
            hands down, did I? Hang on. I know I've got my gun
            somewhere. Would you mind holding this for a moment?
            (He puts his whistle in Gilbert's hand) And can I give
            you this to hold a second?

            > *Grummett puts his notebook in Crosby's hand.*
            > *He continues searching through his pockets,*
            > *looking for his gun, and placing more of his*
            > *personal possessions into the Convicts' hands:*
            > *his wallet, his handkerchief, etc. He produces a*
            > *truncheon.*

            And can I ask you to look after this for one tiny moment?

Crosby   It's a truncheon, Detective Constable Grummett.

Grummett   I know. I'm not supposed to have one really, according
            to the strictest letter of the law. They're more for
            uniformed constables. Only when I'm going home late at
            night, I have to go right past this very spooky churchyard
            —there's like all these owls hooting, there's this wind
            whistling through the bell-tower, there's all these trees
            waving about, it doesn't half give you the colly-wobbles
            —so I always carry a truncheon with me.

Gilbert   I don't blame you.

Grummett   Anyway . . . *(He gives the truncheon to Crosby)* . . .
            where the hummers did I put that gun? I'm sure I had it
            when I left the house this morning. Well, I'm almost
            sure . . . Oh, yes, here . . .

Gilbert   Excuse me, Detective Constable Grummett?

Grummett   Yes?

Gilbert   I think your shoe-lace is undone.

Grummett   I beg your pardon?

            > *Gilbert winks at the audience and scratches his*
            > *nose. The audience yell out 'Your shoe-lace is*
            > *undone'.*

            Is it? Ta very much. I might have had a nasty accident.

            > *Grummett bends down to tie up his shoe-lace*
            > *and Crosby hits him with the truncheon.*

            Ow! Oh! My fizzin' head! That flippin' hurt!

Gilbert   Come on, Crosby, run for it!

Crosby   Where to?

Gilbert   Where we said—we'll run across to where the big posh
           houses are and climb in through a window.

           Gilbert and Crosby take refuge again in the
           audience. Grummett, still rubbing his head,
           recovers sufficiently to pick up his whistle and
           he starts blowing short sharp blasts on it. The
           Warders appear again and Grummett indicates
           the way the fugitives have gone.

Grummett   They're out there somewhere, hiding. After them, lads!

           And the two Warders pursue Crosby and Gilbert
           into the Audience. the Convicts attempt to hide
           in the auditorium, ducking along the aisles
           and behind the rows of seats, entreating the
           audience to help them. The two Warders search
           along the rows, also appealing for the audience's
           help. At the end of this chase sequence, we have
           again lost both Convicts and Warders. We are
           left with Grummett on the stage, recovering
           from his bump on the head.

Grummett   I'm not kidding, I bet there's a lump as big as a duck-egg
           on my head tomorrow morning. That'll be great will
           that, spending Christmas with a big bump on my head!
           I'll spifflicate them convicts when I do lay hold of them.
           It was supposed to be my day off was this. *(He glowers*
           up at the Circle) And I haven't finished with you lot yet,
           not by a long chalk! I'm on my way to get a few more
           names in my little book, among you ones up there in the
           high-rise flats. So you can just stop fidgeting, and fold
           your arms, and sit up straight! I'll teach you to harbour
           missing convicts! I'm on my way, so look out! *(He feels*
           at his head again, gingerly) Flippin' hecky Moses, but it
           doesn't half *hurt*!

           Grummett goes off.

Scene Three

           A living room. There is a Christmas tree, a
           stocking hanging above the fireplace, a few
           Christmas cards on the mantelpiece. The door
           opens slightly, a hand switches on the light, and
           Gilbert peers into the room.

Gilbert   There's nobody here—come on.

Gilbert enters, followed cautiously by Crosby.

Crosby   It's not very posh, is it?

Gilbert   It'll do. It's neat and tidy. I'll say this for it, it's a bit more pleasant than that prison cell.

Crosby   We can't stay here for Christmas though, can we?

Gilbert   We're not staying here for Christmas, we're going to get our breath, we're going to wait until Grummett and his cronies are somewhere else, and then we're on our way again.

Crosby   On our way where to?

Gilbert   I don't know where to, Crosby, I do wish you'd stop going on about where we're going and what we're going to do. I've got you in out of the rain, haven't I? It's warm and dry, isn't it? We've given Grummett and them warders the slip, haven't we? There's nobody in this house at this minute, so make the most of it, man. Sit down and take it easy while you've got the chance.

Crosby   I think I will. My dogs are crippling me.

While Gilbert inspects the room, Crosby sits down, takes off one of his shoes, and rubs at his feet.

Do you want to know what I'm missing right now?

Gilbert   Not particularly.

Crosby   I'll tell you anyway. My bed-time cocoa. I really used to enjoy my bed-time cocoa in that prison cell. I really used to look forward to it.

Gilbert   You always used to complain there was no sugar in it.

Crosby   There wasn't ever any sugar in it, I freely admit that. But I used to drink it, didn't I?

Gilbert   After a lot of fuss.

Crosby   Never mind the fuss, matey, I used to drink it—every drop. And you can't deny that. And I'll tell you something else I've just remembered.

Gilbert   Go on.

Crosby   Last Christmas Eve, if you'll cast your mind back, in the nick, we got a digestive biscuit with our cocoa, didn't we?

Gilbert   Did we?

Crosby   You know very well we did.

Gilbert   So what?

Crosby   So what, he says! I'd give anything for a digestive biscuit right now. I could just enjoy one. I'm starving. My stomach must think my throat's been cut.

> *Gilbert has discovered a bowl containing wrapped sweets and packets of crisps. He tosses a bag of crisps at Crosby.*

Gilbert   Get your choppers round them, then.

Crosby   What's this?

Gilbert   What does it look like? It's a bag of Smokey Bacon crisps.

Crosby   I can't eat these!

Gilbert   Don't you like Smokey Bacon? Would you rather have Roast Chicken or Salt & Vinegar flavour?

> *Crosby stares as though mesmerised at the packet of crisps he is holding and then drops the bag as though it was a hot brick.*

Crosby   I don't want any flavour! What are you trying to do, Gilbert? Are you trying to get us put away for life?

Gilbert   What's the matter now?

Crosby   That's *stealing*, man.

Gilbert   Of course it's stealing, we're criminals, aren't we? It's what we do for a living, isn't it?

Crosby   Yes. But there's no point in sticking our necks out. No sense in taking unnecessary risks.

Gilbert   It's only a bag of fizzin' Smokey Bacon crisps, man!

Crosby   Yes, and it's got our finger-prints all over it. Yours *and* mine. That's evidence now, that bag of crisps. They can produce that in court, if they feel like it. With a little luggage label on it—Exhibit 'A'.

> *Gilbert picks up the bag of crisps and tears it open.*

Gilbert   It won't be Exhibit 'A' when I've done with it.

Crosby   What do you think you're doing now?

Gilbert   Disposing of the evidence.

Crosby   I'm beginning to wish I'd never let you talk me into breaking out of clink.

Gilbert   *(munching a crisp)* Delicious.

Crosby   Because we'll never see the light of day again, you know that, if they ever do catch hold of us.

Gilbert   Are you sure you don't want one?

Crosby   They're very strict with escaped convicts, they come
           down very hard on them—like a ton of bricks. It gives
           the prison a bad name. Then there's this house-breaking
           and entering, that's a serious crime, as well. To say
           nothing of bopping Detective Constable Grummett
           on the head. I shouldn't think they'll take too kindly
           to that.

Gilbert   Have a crisp.

Crosby   I don't want a crisp.

Gilbert   Why not?

Crosby   I wouldn't touch one if you paid me.

Gilbert   You're afraid to eat one.

Crosby   No, I'm not.

Gilbert   Yes, you are.

Crosby   No, I'm not.

Gilbert   Oh, yes you are! *(Appealing to the Audience)* He is,
           isn't he?

Crosby   I'm not, am I?

Gilbert   Oh, yes he is!

Crosby   Oh, no I'm not!

Gilbert   You're terrified! You're shaking like a jelly-baby in a
           thunderstorm. *(He proffers his crisps to children in the
           front row of the stalls)* You'll have one, won't you? Will
           you have one? How about you? *(Back to Crosby)* There
           you are, you see—it's only you that's scared to touch
           them.

Crosby   I just don't happen to fancy a crisp, not at this particular
           moment, that's all. That's fair enough, isn't it? I just
           don't happen to be all that keen on crisps—I've never
           been a very big crisp eater.

                    *Gilbert has picked up the bowl containing all
                    the packets of crisps and the wrapped sweets:
                    he proffers it to Crosby.*

Gilbert   Have a sweetie instead.

Crosby   No thanks.

Gilbert   Go on—they're nice ones.

Crosby   I'd rather not.

Gilbert   Why not?

Crosby	I'm not all that bothered about sweets and toffees either. I never have been. It's a well-known fact. Ask anybody.
Gilbert	You're frightened to touch them, aren't you?
Crosby	Of course I'm not! Don't talk ridiculous. *(Brandishing his fist)* I'll get you, Gilbert, I mean that, if you talk like that—I don't care if you are the only pal I've got. I'll really duff you up, I will, I'm not kidding.
Gilbert	Suit yourself. If you don't want them, I'll find somebody that does. *(He addresses the audience)* All right then, who wants some sweets and crisps? Don't all shout at once.

> *And Gilbert tosses the sweets and crisps out into the audience.*

There you are—that's it—that's the lot.

Crosby	They weren't yours to give away, I hope you realise that.
Gilbert	I don't care whose they were.
Crosby	You might have cause to regret that, I'm only telling you.

> *Crosby remains seated, rubbing his aching feet, while Gilbert does another inspection of the room.*

Gilbert   I must say, it's a nice house, isn't it? I like the wallpaper.
          I like the decorations. I like the Chrissy tree, as well—it's
          a pretty one, isn't it? You can't beat a real tree, can you
          —I don't like the artificial ones. Hey, Crosby, will you
          look at this! I've seen some sights in my time, but I've
          never seen anything to beat this! Just have a guess at
          what there is underneath the Chrissy tree as a present
          for somebody?

Crosby   I've no idea.

Gilbert   I know you've no idea—I want you to try and guess.

Crosby   Is it a toy farmyard with cows and sheep and pigs and a
          plastic milkmaid with two titchy buckets hanging round
          her neck?

Gilbert   No, guess again.

Crosby   I can't—I can't think of anything else.

Gilbert   *Try*, man. Don't be a spoil-sport, Cros, have one more
          guess.

Crosby   Is it a big box of soldiers, goodjuns and badjuns, and a
          fort with a drawbridge.

Gilbert   You're getting colder.

Crosby   I give up.

Gilbert   *(holding up his discovery)* How about these then? You
          wouldn't have guessed these in a million trillion years.
          A pair of size fourteen boots! Who'd want a pair of size
          fourteen boots for a Chrissy present?

Crosby   I don't know.

Gilbert   Neither do I!

Crosby   A policeman with big feet, perhaps.

                    *Gilbert pauses to study the boots, one in each
                    hand, uneasily.*

Gilbert   Hey, that's a thought. I never thought of that. *(He sets
          the boots down again, neatly)* Look, there's another
          prezzy here that's not been wrapped up. A shiny bright
          whistle.

Crosby   That's another present for a constable.

Gilbert   *(picking up a large box)* And how about a Bumper
          Disguise Outfit, complete with false nose and ginger
          beard? Who would you say that was for?

Crosby   A Detective Constable.

Gilbert   Don't tell me—we haven't, have we?

Crosby   Haven't what, Gilbert?

Gilbert   We haven't broken into whose house I think we've
           broken into?

Crosby   Why? Whose house do you think we've broken into?

Gilbert   I don't like to think of it. Just a minute. *(He crosses
           to the mantelpiece and takes down a Christmas card)*
           I'll have a look at who this Chrissy card's addressed to.
           *(He looks at the picture on the front first, and pulls a
           face)* Just look at this Santa Claus on the front, will you!
           He looks as if he's been drawn by a two-year-old kid
           with a blunt clothes-prop. *(He looks inside the card,
           pauses, then:)* Crosby?

Crosby   What is it, Gilbert?

Gilbert   Can I ask you a question?

Crosby   Of course.

Gilbert   Did you by any chance send Detective Constable
           Grummett a Christmas card this year?

Crosby   Of course I did. I always do. Every year. I draw one
           and paint it myself. But I never put my name on it. I
           send it anon . . . anono . . . anono-what-is-it?

Gilbert   Anonymously.

Crosby   That's it.

Gilbert   *(reading the card's inscription)* 'I hate you, Detective
           Constable Grummett, I really hate you, Happy Xmas,
           signed, your enemy.'

Crosby   Hey, that's exactly the same as I wrote in my card! *(He
           turns and looks at the card as Gilbert holds it up)* That
           is my card—that's the Santa I drew and painted! What's
           it doing here?

Gilbert   We *have* done it. We've broken into Detective Constable
           Grummett's house. Of all the luck!

Crosby   That doesn't prove we have, Gilbert.

Gilbert   Of course it does!

Crosby   Not at all. Not by any means. That's my card to
          Detective Constable Grummett, yes—but the postman
          could have put it through the wrong letter-box.

Gilbert   I'll try another one then. *(He replaces the card, picks up
          another one, and reads the inscription)* 'To Detective
          Constable Grummett and family, from his loving mum,
          kiss, kiss, kiss, kiss, kiss.'

Crosby   Funny that—somehow you never think of Detective
          Constable Grummett having a mum.

Gilbert   One more. *(And he reads from yet another card)* 'Upon
          this sprig of holly, Two robins you will find, They bring
          you cheer and tidings, Of peace to all mankind.'

Crosby   That's nice.

Gilbert   'To Detective Constable Grummett and family from
          Geoffrey and Susan and all at number thirty-seven.'

Crosby   I wonder who they are?

Gilbert   It doesn't matter who they are, Crosby, you daft dozy
          lump! It goes to prove that we are definitely in
          Grummett's house! Right?

Crosby   There's no need to shout at me, Gilbert. Keep your wig
          on.

Gilbert   I'll shout if I want! It's enough to make anybody shout!
          Of all the rotten luck! Trust us! What's Detective
          Constable Grummett going to say when he finds out?
          When he adds up all the things we've done to him?
          We've bopped him on the nut. We've broken into and
          entered his house. We've eaten his crisps *and* his sweets.
          You know what he *is* going to think? He's going to
          think that we've done it all on purpose, isn't he? He's
          going to think that we've got it in for him.

Crosby   Yes, and whose idea was it to pinch his crisps and his
          sweets? Not mine.

Gilbert   Never mind whose idea it was.

Crosby   It's all right you saying 'never mind', but I advised you
          not to do it. Specifically. But you had to be the clever
          one. Pinching a Detective Constable's sweeties, and
          eating his crisps. You could probably get fifteen years
          apiece for both of those charges.

Gilbert   I didn't eat them all myself, did I? *(He indicates the audience)* They helped me—they're just as much to blame as I am.

Crosby   They'll probably get fifteen years apiece as well.

Gilbert   Not if we put things right, they won't. We'll put the room back exactly as it was when we came here, and then we'll clear off out of it, before Grummett turns up.

Crosby   How can you put the crisps and toffees back where they were? You haven't got them to put back.

Gilbert   I can get them back. *(He addresses the audience)* Will all those children who accepted crisps or sweeties, not knowing them to be the property of Detective Constable Grummett, C.I.D., when I threw them out, please throw them back again. *(Pause)* At once. *(Pause)* This instant. *(Pause)* Immediately. *(Pause)* Now. *(Pause, then pleading)* Come on, kids, this is no joke, you know. We'll all be in serious hot water. He'll go spare will Detective Constable Grummett, if he comes back here and finds all his Chrissie crisps and sweeties missing. So let's have them back eh? And the sooner you sling them back, the sooner Crosby and me can put this room straight and naff off out of it.

Crosby   Perhaps they haven't got them.

Gilbert   Of course they've got them—I gave them to them.

Crosby   They might have had them then yes, but that doesn't mean they've got them now. They might have eaten them.

Gilbert   Oh crikey! What can we do?

Crosby   Don't look at me. It wasn't my idea to take them in the first place, was it?

Gilbert   So you keep saying.

Crosby   It was your idea. You get these mad ideas in your head and you won't listen to reason. I hate you sometimes, Gilbert, when you get your mad ideas. I do—I really hate you.

Gilbert   Never mind now whose idea it was or wasn't. What we've got to decide is what we're going to do about it. *(He appeals to the audience)* Listen, kids—all those of you that have eaten a sweet or one of Detective Constable Grummett's tattie crisps, pay special attention—we have to think of something. Because if Detective Constable Grummett turns nasty, which he's more than capable of doing, he could have every one of you X-rayed, and that *would* cause problems. And we haven't got much time because he might walk into this room at any moment.

Crosby   Do you mind if I make a suggestion?

Gilbert   Not at all. I'd be grateful.

Crosby   How's this, then? Could we have the house lights up, please? Right up? *(The house lights go on)* Thank you. *(He addresses the audience)* Right then. All those of you who have swallowed a crisp or a sweet or a toffee this afternoon, put your hands up.

Gilbert   Just a minute. You mean, all those who have swallowed one of Detective Constable Grummett's crisps or sweets or toffees, don't you?

Crosby   Not at all. I mean *any* kind of sweet or crisp or toffee. Bought, begged, borrowed or stolen. Because if Grummett goes to work with his C.I.D. X-ray machine, you don't imagine that the sweets and toffees inside kiddies' tummies are going to have Detective Constable Grummett's name on them, do you?

Gilbert   I never thought of that.

Crosby   You never think of anything, that's half your trouble. That's why I'm telling you—anybody with any kind of sweet *or* crisp *or* toffee *or* chocolate, or any other kind of goodie lodged in his or her stomach, is definitely going to be guilty as far as Grummett is concerned, no danger.

Gilbert   What are we going to do about it?

Crosby   That's what I'm trying to organise, if you'll just shut up and listen. Hands up again all those who have swallowed sweeties, crisps or chocolates this afternoon, no matter where they got them.

Gilbert   There's quite a lot of them, isn't there?

Crosby   Didn't you expect that there would be? All right then, kiddies, this is what Uncle Crosby wants you to do. Turn round and ask whoever you came with—your dad or your mum or your auntie or whoever—to give you twenty pence. Then, when I say the word, I want you all to nip into the foyer and buy yourselves a bag of suckers, or a bar of chocolate, or a packet of boiled sweeties, or anything at all like that from one of the attendants. Then, when you've got your sweeties, run

round and leave them at the stage door, and the stage
door keeper will have them sent up here to us.

Gilbert   That's a great idea, Crosby.

Crosby   Do you like it?

Gilbert   I do. I think it's really terrific. Because if everybody gets
             a bag of sweets or something we'll have more than
             enough to fill Grummett's bowl, won't we?

Crosby   Ample.

Gilbert   And anything that's left over, we could hang on to,
             make it last out for all the rest of the performances this
             week, couldn't we?

Crosby   Of course we could.

Gilbert   And it would be good to have a bit put by in case we
             get a stingy audience like we had in yesterday.

Crosby   Right—they were a lot of meanies, weren't they? I hate
             mean people, Gilbert. I do—I really hate them.

Gilbert   This lot don't look mean, though. They look quite
             generous.

Crosby   All right then, children, get your twenty pence from
             whoever you came with. Don't forget your manners,
             ask them nicely. But if they won't give you the money
             when you've been polite, you have my permission to
             duff them up.

Gilbert   Don't say that, Crosby!

Crosby   Why not? We're supposed to be villainous evil rascals,
             aren't we? What we can't achieve by fair means, we
             achieve by foul! Go on, kids, get stuck in!

                         *Over the above, the living room door has opened
                         slowly and Alexander Grummett, Detective
                         Constable Grummett's schoolboy son, has
                         tiptoed in. Alexander Grummett is an obnoxious
                         lanky ruffian. He wears a grubby pullover
                         over his pyjamas. He is carrying a pea-shooter in
                         one hand and a revolver in the other. Unnoticed
                         by Gilbert and Crosby, whose attentions are
                         directed at the audience, Alexander tip-toes
                         closer to them. He puts his pea-shooter up to
                         his mouth and fires first at the back of Gilbert's
                         neck.*

Gilbert   Oooh!

And immediately, Alexander fires again, this time at the back of Crosby's neck:

Crosby   Ow!

The convicts rub their necks and turn, surprised, and look at Alexander.

Alexander   Got you both red-handed! Hands up!

Crosby   Be careful, son, with that pea-shooter. It hurt, did that!

Gilbert   I'll say—right on the back of my neck!

Alexander   Reach for the sky, before I blast you full of holes! Ker*boom*! Ker*boom*!

Gilbert   Just a minute, sonny. *(He calls out to the back of the auditorium)* Could we have the lights out, please?

The house lights, which went on when Gilbert and Crosby were addressing the audience, go down again.

Now then, my little chap, is it a game? What's happening? Are you the goodie and are we the baddies? But we mustn't fire our pea-shooter at the backs of nice kind gentlemen's necks, must we, because it hurts them.

Crosby   No, and the nice kind gentlemen might duff us up if we hurt them, right?

Alexander   It was meant to hurt. And this'll hurt as well. This'll do more than hurt. This'll blow your heads off, this gun. Ker*pow*! Ker*boom*! Kersplatt!

Gilbert   Yes, we'd like to stop and play with you, young man. Join you in your little game. But we just called in to see your mummy or your daddy. They must have left the front door open when they went out. And as your mummy and your daddy aren't at home, we'll have to go away—won't we?—and come back another time. I'm sorry if we woke you up. It's time all little boys were tucked up in their beddy-byes. Now, why don't you put your water-pistol back in the toy-cupboard and go back upstairs to noddies?

Crosby   Up the stairs to Bedfordshire.

Gilbert   The Land of Dreams.

Alexander   It's not a water-pistol this, it's real!

Crosby   It isn't, is it?

Alexander   It is. Ker*sping*! Ker*sping*! Ker*spow*! It's a real police gun. It belongs to my dad, does this.

Gilbert   Detective Constable Grummett?

Alexander   Yeh, he's great. He's the greatest catcher of baddies in the world, my dad, Detective Constable Grummett. He shoots the heads off baddies like you with this gun— kermash, kermash! Then there's blood all over the walls. Ker*splash*! Blood all over the floor and walls.

Crosby   *(shuddering distastefully)* Ugh!

Gilbert   I don't think you ought to wave that gun about, young man, it might go off.

Alexander   It will if I pull this trigger—and I will if either of you move. Ker*poo*! Ker*pow*!

Gilbert   Do you know what time it is?

Alexander   Don't know.

Gilbert   It's very late.

Alexander   Don't care.

Gilbert   You ought to care. It's Christmas Eve, you know. And you know who comes down that chimney, when *good* little boys are fast asleep?

Crosby   Santa Claus.

Gilbert   Santa Claus. Right.

Alexander	If anybody comes down that chimney now he gets it in his whiskers—Ker*pow*! Ker*pow*!
Gilbert	What's your name, little chap?
Alexander	Mind your own business or you'll get it now—Ker*boom*! Ker*boom*!
Gilbert	My name's Gilbert. And his is Crosby.
Crosby	Crosby.
Gilbert	Only if you like you can call us Uncle Gilbert and Uncle Crosby.
Crosby	If you want to.
Alexander	Shut up. Don't talk. I'm going to keep you standing here until my dad gets home. And then I'm going to tell him that you tried to bash me up but I managed to overpower you.
Gilbert	Uncle Crosby?
Crosby	Yes, Uncle Gilbert?
Gilbert	I'm going to try and—er—you know.
Crosby	What's that?
Gilbert	*You* know. I—er—you know, and then you—er—you know—like we did before.
Crosby	No, I don't know, Gilbert.
Alexander	Shut up.
Gilbert	Yes, you *do* know. *(With his hands up in the air, he tries to mime scratching his nose)* I scratch my—you know—and they shout—you know—and then he bends down and—you know—and then you know—like you did before.
Crosby	*(the light dawns slowly)* Oh, that! *I* know! Great, Gilbert. Fantastic!
Gilbert	Young man, I say, do you mind if I bring my hand down low enough to scratch my nose. It's itching.
Alexander	You aren't going to try and get me with that old your-shoe-lace-is-undone trick, are you? That's ancient, that one. It's as old as the hills. I knew it ages ago.
Gilbert	Of course not.
Crosby	No.
Alexander	I think I'll tell my dad, when he comes home, that you tried to drown me in the bath, but I managed to get the better of you both with a double-reverse leg-lock and a Japanese strangle-hold.

Gilbert   Oh, quick, look behind you! There's a horrible hairy spider coming down from the ceiling!

Crosby   Where is it, Gilbert?

Gilbert   Up there!

Crosby   I can't see it.

Gilbert   Yes, you can! It's right above his head!

Crosby   No. I can't.

Gilbert   You can! It's just like the one in the prison cell! The one we had to call the warders about!

Crosby   *(again the light dawns, slowly)* Oh! *That* spider! Oh yes, I can see it now! It's all hairy and horrible!

Gilbert   With long straggly legs all twisting up and wriggling about!

Crosby   Ugh, take it away, take it away, I don't like it!

Alexander *(without moving)* Shut up, both of you! That's even older than your-shoe-lace-is-undone trick, is that one. You don't think you're going to catch me with the horrible-hairy-spider gag, do you? One more sound out of either of you—one more mention of the word 'spider' —and you really will get it this time. K*apow!* K*apow!* K*apow!*

> *Gilbert and Crosby keep their mouths shut tight. And now the horrible hairy spider does appear, coming down directly above Alexander's head. He does not notice it. As the spider dangles above Alexander's head, Gilbert and Crosby shudder and writhe with horror, performing various facial contortions, but unable to utter a word for fear of being shot.*

Alexander Stand still and don't move!

> *At last, the spider returns to where it came from, to the relief of Gilbert and Crosby, and without Alexander ever having been aware of its existence.*

Gilbert   Crosby!

Crosby   What?

Gilbert   I thought I saw the door-handle move.

Crosby   That's funny, so did I.

Alexander That's the oldest one of all. You won't get me with one as old as that, it's got whiskers on it. It's even older than the your-shoe-lace-is-undone trick *and* the horrible-hairy-spider gag. It's older than both of them put together is the moving-door-handle-one.

> *Gilbert and Crosby continue to stare at the door, fascinated, as the door-handle does move, and the events listed by Alexander below take place.*

Gilbert There it goes again!

Crosby It's definitely moving is that door-handle, it's turning round!

Alexander And I suppose you're going to tell me that the door is opening?

Gilbert}
Crosby} It is, it is—however did you guess?

Alexander Slowly creaking open wider?

Gilbert}
Crosby} Yes, you're right!

Alexander And now, I suppose, a sinister gloved hand is creeping into the room?

Gilbert That's exactly what is happening!

Crosby You must have eyes in the back of your head!

Alexander And now, I suppose, it's feeling for the light switch?

Gilbert I don't know how he does it!

Crosby It's like second sight—some people are born like it!

Alexander And I suppose it's just about to plunge us into pitch darkness?

> *At which point, the gloved hand on the light switch does plunge the room into pitch darkness. We hear shots, shouts, and the sound of a scuffle, then:*

Gilbert Crosby! Crosby! Help me, help me!

Crosby I've got him, Gilbert! I've got him in my special thumb-hold so he can't escape!

Gilbert I think there's more than one of him—'cause somebody's got me.

Crosby Hang on. Fight back. I'll try and drag my one across to the light switch and then give you a hand.

> *More scuffling, and then the light is switched on. Crosby, at the light switch, is grappling with Gilbert. There is no sign of Alexander. Crosby*

is holding Gilbert in his 'special' thumb-hold, and Gilbert is in agony.

Gilbert   Ow!—Oooooh!—Ahhh!—Eeeeh!

Crosby, realising his mistake, releases Gilbert.

Crosby   Sorry, Gilbert.

Gilbert, lost for words, puts his thumbs under his armpits and walks around for a while.

I didn't realise it was you, otherwise I wouldn't have bent your thumbs back so far, if I'd known. I thought you were somebody else.

Gilbert   *(picking up the gun from the floor)* I said it was a water pistol. *(He fires it in Crosby's face)* It is, you know.

Crosby   Careful—you want to look what you're doing!

Gilbert   So do you! Be sure whose thumbs you're holding next time.

Crosby   I will. I'll try.

Gilbert   Where's young Grummett gone?

Crosby   I don't know. And to be perfectly honest, Gilbert, I don't really care all that much either. I wasn't exactly struck on him—I didn't like his attitude. He reminded me of his dad, in many ways, Detective Constable Grummett.

Gilbert   I wonder who switched the light out?

Crosby   I don't know that either.

Gilbert   Look—what's that?

Gilbert indicates a large note that is propped up on the mantelpiece.

Crosby   It wasn't there before whoever it was switched the light out, Gilbert. It's not another Chrissy card, is it?

Gilbert   *(taking down the note)* It's a message. It's addressed to Detective Constable Grummett.

Crosby	Perhaps we shouldn't read it then. We're in enough trouble as it is.
Gilbert	It's a kidnap note!
Crosby	Has somebody kidnapped Detective Constable Grummett, Gilbert?
Gilbert	No, they've kidnapped that lad, his son.
Crosby	*(finding it hard to hide his pleasure at the news)* They haven't, have they? Who? The rotten dogs.
Gilbert	It doesn't say. 'Dear Detective Constable and Missis Grummett. We have kidnapped your son. Do not attempt to follow us. Do not attempt to contact the police. Do nothing until you hear from us. We will let you know.'
Crosby	Is that all it says?
Gilbert	Isn't it enough?
Crosby	It doesn't say 'Yours sincerely' or 'Compliments of the Season' at the end, or anything like that? *(Gilbert shakes his head)* I wonder what they mean?
Gilbert	Who?
Crosby	The Kidnappers. 'We will let you know.' Let us know what?
Gilbert	Not us. Detective Constable and Mrs. Grummett. They'll let them know how much ransom money they want and where to leave it and all like that.
Crosby	Hecky thump!
Gilbert	I shouldn't think they'll get a lot of change out of Detective Constable Grummett, he's not noted for being the most generous of men.
Crosby	They wouldn't get a lot of change out of me if he was my lad.
Gilbert	Blood's thicker than water, Crosby.
Crosby	What's that got to do with it?
Gilbert	It's a saying.
Crosby	Custard's thicker than ginger beer, but I don't see that there's any need to mention it.
Gilbert	I'm merely trying to point out that the boy is Detective Constable Grummett's only son. And that he'll come down like a ton of bricks on the kidnappers, if he ever feels their collars.
Crosby	That's not our worry, is it? We're not them.

Gilbert   Maybe not. But Detective Constable Grummett is going to think it's us.

Crosby   Us? Me and you? Kidnappers?

Gilbert   That's what Detective Constable Grummett's going to think.

Crosby   Why should he?

Gilbert   Of course he will. Consider the situation, from his point of view. Study the facts. Examine all the clues. Sift the evidence. Who escaped from prison?

Crosby   We did.

Gilbert   Who bopped Detective Constable Grummett on the nut?

Crosby   We did.

Gilbert   Who broke into and entered Detective Constable Grummett's house? *And* left their fingerprints all over his walls and furniture?

Crosby   We did.

Gilbert   Who pinched Detective Constable Grummett's Chrissy goodies? All his crisps and sweets?

Crosby   *(pointing to the audience)* They did.

Gilbert   And us.

Crosby   You maybe, not me.

Gilbert   *Us*, Crosby.

Crosby   Oh no, you can't go putting that onto me.

Gilbert   I'm not. I'm only telling you what Detective Constable Grummett is going to think. That we ate his crisps and his sweeties and that it was us that kidnapped his kid. He's bound to think it.

Crosby   That settles it. Come on.

Gilbert   Where to?

Crosby   We're going back to that prison. We're going to give ourselves up.

Gilbert   Back to that cold cell for Christmas Day? Back to that prison chicken dinner? A mingy stingy bit of stringy chicken, clammy sprouts, lumpy spuds and greasy gravy? I should cocoa.

Crosby   It might be different this year.

Gilbert   It won't.

Crosby   It might be—you never know, there might even be a Christmas cracker with it.

Gilbert   There's no crackers. You live in a dream-world. There never is.

Crosby   We've got to go back. We've got to tell Detective Constable Grummett that it wasn't us.

Gilbert   Yes, and he'll believe us, won't he? Please Detective Constable Grummett, we admit that we broke out of prison, we admit that we bopped you on the nut, we admit that we are guilty of breaking and entering your dwelling place *and* noshing all your Chrissy goodies—but it wasn't us that kidnapped your lad. Oh yes, that's vibrant with the ring of truth. He'll believe every word of that, coming from two escaped gaol-birds. You what? You wouldn't be halfway through that yarn before you'd be—crash bang clang—locked up again in that cell. And there'll be no Christmas crackers in there tomorrow, tosher, believe you me! Christmas crackers? In clink? Give over! You'll be lucky if you see a walnut.

Crosby   Can we send somebody else?

Gilbert   How do you mean?

Crosby   To tell them that it wasn't us?

Gilbert   We don't *know* anybody else. I only know you. You only know me. Apart from one or two casual friends, and all of them are doing time. Wait a minute!

Crosby   What?

Gilbert   I've just had a brilliant idea!

Crosby   Not again.

Gilbert   You'll like this one—really. We'll go in disguise. They won't know it's us. We'll go ourselves but as two other fellers. We'll say to them—listen to this:

Crosby   I'm listening.

Gilbert   We have come here today as private citizens —

Crosby   We have come here today as private citizens —

Gilbert   — because we have evidence concerning the kidnapping of Detective Constable Grummett's kiddy —

Crosby   — because we have evidence concerning the kidnapping of Detective Constable Grummett's kiddy —

Gilbert   — It was not convicts Gilbert and Crosby that done it.

Crosby   — It was not convicts Gilbert and Crosby that done it. There's just one thing, Gilbert?

Gilbert   What's that?

Crosby	Where are we going to get these disguises from?
Gilbert	Dead simple. Here. *(And he picks up the bumper disguise kit from underneath the Christmas tree)* We'll borrow Grummett's Chrissy prezzy disguise outfit.
Crosby	I knew it. The minute you said you had an idea, I knew there'd be trouble.
Gilbert	*(opening the box)* He can have it back as soon as we've finished with it. Stop moithering, Crosby. Stick that on, son.

> *Gilbert gives Crosby the ginger beard and himself puts on the false nose complete with spectacles.*

	How do I look?
Crosby	Great. It suits you. How about me?
Gilbert	Yes, you look—well—different.

> *At which point, Clara Grummett, Detective Constable Grummett's wife enters. Clara Grummett is an excitable and voluble woman.*

Clara	Just what has been going on here, if you don't mind me asking, but I do happen to live here. I've only been down as far as the Bingo Hall I come back, there's the hall

light been left on, blazing away, there's the landing light been left on, there's a light on in our Alexander's bedroom, there's a light been left on in the lavvy—I'm not kidding—you get halfway up the street and this house looks like Blackpool Illuminations. What's going on? And who's been moving them Christmas cards about on top of the mantelpiece—some people can't keep their hands off nothing. And who are you two, if you'll pardon the question? And what are you doing in my living room?

Gilbert Bona fide employees of the Gas Board, ma'am, who chanced to be passing—so we thought we'd snatch at opportunity and read your meter. Mrs. Grummett is it?

Clara I sincerely hope so.

Gilbert Mrs. Grummett, as well as clocking your meter, we are also here as private citizens —

Crosby Private citizens —

Gilbert We have evidence concerning the kidnapping of your kiddy —

Crosby Your kiddy —

Clara What kidnapping? Which kiddy? Not my Alexander, not my only one? Where is he? Where is my precious baby? If he's got out of that bed again, without asking, I shall kill him. I will, I'll slaughter him—I don't care if it is Christmas!

Gilbert *(handing her the note)* Read that, ma'am. And take our word for it, it was not convicts Gilbert and Crosby that done it. Come on, Crosby son, scarper!

> *As Clara Grummett studies the note, Gilbert and Crosby take the opportunity to leave. Clara comes to the end of the note, and:*

Clara My little Alexander! My precious one, my baby! Bring him back, I want my little darling-heart, my tiny chick-a-biddy! Help! Help! Kidnappers! Murderers! Thieves!

> *Clara rushes out of the room and off the stage still shouting. As Clara goes off at one side, Detective Constable Grummett enters from the other, and addresses the audience, sternly.*

Grummett Right, then, sit up straight, no talking. I have to inform you that a serious crime has been committed and, as an officer of New Scotland Yard, it is my duty to apprehend and arrest the criminal. I'm talking to you big ones now, not the children. One of you has left a car parked, outside this theatre, for a period exceeding an hour and a half in an area where waiting time is strictly limited to thirty minutes. I don't know how you manage to do it—there is a sign up—it's big enough! *(He brandishes his notebook)* I have the number of the offending vehicle jotted down in my notebook, and if the owner doesn't move it within the next ten minutes, the due processes of the machinery of the law will be set in motion. You'll find yourself going home on the tube, if you take my meaning.

> *At which point, Clara rushes on-stage,*
> *still carrying the kidnap note.*

Clara   Stephen, Stephen! How glad I am I've found you! I've been searching everywhere—distraught and at my wits end because of the vile and evil thing that has happened!

Grummett   Clara, how many times must I have to tell you not to bother me when I'm on duty?

Clara   *(thrusting the note into his hand)* Read that—read it, my husband, and then tell me I did wrong to seek you out! Read it, and then wonder at the wicked minds that should concoct such an awful ghastly crime!

Grummett   *(studies the note)* This is serious. This is very serious indeed.

Clara   What can we do? Are we going to meet their extortionate demands? What *are* their extortionate demands? Who can we turn to in this, our hour of tragedy? What are we going to do?

Grummett   Don't you worry, Clara. The entire resources of New Scotland Yard will be at our disposal. We'll get little Alexander back, safe and unharmed.

Clara   It says in the note that we mustn't attempt to contact the police.

Grummett   But I *am* the police. Where did you get this note?

Clara   From two bona fide employees of the Gas Board—they happened to be passing so they called in and read our meter.

Grummett   That sounds fishy for a start. Can you describe these bona fide Gas Board employees?

Clara   Yes—one of them had a ginger beard and the other one had a big red conk and wore glasses. Do you think they might have been impostors?

Grummett It's possible. I don't know what to think, right now. I've
had a hell of a day. There's two dangerous convicts
escaped. I've been bopped on the nut by one of them.
There's a member or members of the audience parked up
illegally. There's a horrible hairy spider comes into it
somewhere. And now this—my own son kidnapped. I
need time to think and sort things out.

Clara But Stephen, *is* there time—is time not on *their* side?

Grummett Go home, Clara. Leave it all to me.

Clara If that's what you think best, Stephen.

Grummett I do. The kidnappers may want to contact you. Go home,
sit by the telephone, do not move. And don't worry,
Clara.

> *Clara nods and goes off. Grummett flicks
> through his notebook and licks the end of
> his pencil, and addresses the audience:*

Grummett This gets worse and worse. Helping convicts to escape.
Parking cars illegally. Being cheeky. Kidnapping my son,
Alexander. You could be here all night. I shall suspend
all activities up here on the stage for fifteen minutes,
while I come down there and interview a lot more
suspects. You will all sit tight. Except for those persons
who have ginger beards, big red conks, or possess a car
with the registration number, XKB 4982. Will anybody
in any of those categories meet me in the foyer?
Meanwhile, two senior Scotland Yard officials will pass
among you, disguised as ice-cream ladies selling orange
drinks and lollies. Behave yourselves.

> *Grummett strides off-stage.*

END OF ACT ONE

ACT TWO
Scene One

A POLICE STATION

Warder Mullins is behind the desk, writing in the station log book. Detective Constable Grummett walks onto the stage, carrying a rolled-up poster underneath his arm, and addresses the audience.

Grummett Right then, sit up straight and pay attention, where were we? Two dangerous convicts, Gilbert and Crosby, have escaped from prison. A horrible hairy spider is known to be loitering with intent to commit a mischief. A car parked illegally, registration number XKB 4982, has been towed away on my authority. My son, Alexander Grummett, has been kidnapped by a person or persons unknown but possibly masquerading as bona fide employees of the Gas Board. During the interval, a small boy sitting in Row J of the stalls, named Kevin Docherty, has been searched and found to have a false moustache in his possession. He claims to have got it out of a lucky bag! And I thought I'd heard everything! The boy, Kevin Docherty, has been taken to New Scotland Yard where he is now helping the police with their enquiries. Carrying on from there . . . *(He moves towards the Police Station, but pauses)* By the way, leaving litter lying about is a punishable offence—so when you've finished with those ice-cream tubs, don't stick them under the seat. Put them in mum's handbag or dad's overcoat pocket.

And now he does go into the Police Station.

Mullins 'Ow do, Detective Constable Grummett.

Grummett 'Ow do.

Mullins Or should I say, Merry Christmas?

Grummett Compliments of the season.

Mullins What's the latest news on the missing convicts?

Grummett Not a lot.

Mullins And what about the kidnapping of Grummett Junior?

Grummett Not a lot to report there either, as yet. Except to state that we are leaving no stone unturned and searching every possible avenue with a fine-tooth comb in our efforts to apprehend the wrong-doers.

Mullins   I thought you might be. I hear that you've taken in a member of the audience for questioning.

Grummett   Yes, but only a little one. *(He produces a false moustache and hands it to the warder)* He was found with this in his trouser pocket. It's a false moustache.

> *The Warder examines the moustache and shakes his head, sadly.*

Mullins   It's not the sort of thing that you expect from members of the audience, is it?

Grummett   I sometimes think it's the times we live in.

Mullins   You don't have to tell me. My father played in pantomime all over the United Kingdom before he retired. He was Wishee-Washee at the Bradford Alhambra; he was Baron Hardup at the Glasgow Empire—there was never so much as a sniff of trouble from the audience. Never.

Grummett   He sounds an interesting old cove. Is he still with us?

Mullins   Hale and hearty, eighty-two years old, and living in a bed-sit in Kennington. He once played the Leeds City Palace of Varieties—he's got posters to prove it.

Grummett   Really? You must tell me more about him, sometime, only I'm hot on the trail of our Alexander's kidnappers. Oh, speaking of posters—stick this up on the wall for me, would you?

> *And Grummett hands his rolled-up poster to the Warder and exits.*
>
> *Warder Mullins examines the false moustache that Grummett has left behind, and tries it on.*

> *Gilbert and Crosby enter, wearing the ginger beard and the false nose, and pause before going into the Police Station.*

Gilbert   Go on then, Crosby, in you go.

Crosby   You first, Gilbert.

Gilbert   Let's have a practice. We have come here as private citizens —

Crosby   Private citizens —

Gilbert   We have evidence concerning the kidnapping of Detective Constable Grummett's kiddy —

Crosby   Constable Grummett's kiddy —

Gilbert   It was not convicts Gilbert and Crosby that done it.

Crosby   Done it.

Gilbert   Fair enough, in we go.

Crosby   You're sure it's safe?

Gilbert   Of course it's safe.

Crosby   Supposing they recognise us?

Gilbert   In these disguises?

Crosby   They might see through them.

Gilbert   I doubt it.

Crosby   What if they do?

Gilbert   The same as before—we'll run for it. Give them the slip and break in somewhere. Does that answer your question? *(Crosby nods)* In you go.

Crosby   Gilbert?

Gilbert   What is it?

Crosby   If we do have to run for it, and if we do break in somewhere—could it, please, not be Detective Constable Grummett's house this time that we break into?

Gilbert   We'll try not to. We'll do our best not to make the same mistake again. Forward.

> *And Gilbert and Crosby, wearing the ginger beard and the spectacles with the false nose, walk into the Police Station where, behind the desk, stands Warder Mullins, wearing the false moustache.*

Mullins   'Ow do?

Gilbert   Good evening.

Mullins   Or may I say Merry Christmas?

Crosby	And a Very Happy New Year to you.
Mullins	Thank you. What can I do you for?
Gilbert	We have come here as private citizens —
Crosby	Private citizens —
Mullins	Just a minute. *(He studies them closely)* Have we ever met before?
Gilbert	I don't think so.
Mullins	Your face suddenly seemed to look familiar. *(to Crosby)* Have you always had a beard? *(Crosby nods)* Have you always worn glasses and had a big red conk?
Gilbert	As long as I can remember.
Mullins	Funny. I must be mistaken, but I seldom forget a face—well, it pays not to in this job—and I could have sworn I'd seen you two before somewhere not long ago.
Crosby	Now that you come to mention it, you know, your face looks familiar.
Mullins	There you are! I wonder where it could have been.
Gilbert	Would it have been in the Gas Board?
Mullins	Could it have been?
Crosby	Why should it have been?
Gilbert	It might have been. We are both bona fide Gas Board employees.
Crosby	Of course we are!
Mullins	That's where it was then. I was in the Gas Board only last week. I went in to pay my bill. Haven't the prices gone up? My word! Do you know, I've got one little gas-ring, that's all. Well, I don't do a lot of cooking. I live on my own. Anyway, how much did it come to? I forget now. But that must have been where I've seen you. The Gas Board. What was it you said you wanted?
Gilbert	We have come here as private citizens —
Crosby	Private citizens —
Mullins	Excuse me, but could you just hang on a moment? Only there's something I promised to do for one of our Detective Constables.
	Warder Mullins hangs up the poster that Grummett gave him on the wall behind his desk. It is a large Police Wanted Poster headed 'WANTED FOR KIDNAPPING' and showing the identikit type portraits of two men, one

wearing a ginger beard and the other a big red nose and glasses. The Warder studies the poster.

Mullins   There we are. *(And he turns back to Gilbert and Crosby)* You were saying?

Gilbert   We have come here as private citizens —

Crosby   Private citizens —

Something is nagging at the back of the Warder's mind.

Mullins   Just a minute.

Warder Mullins turns and studies the poster again, he turns back and studies the faces of Gilbert and Crosby. Then, once more, turns back back to look at the poster. Gilbert and Crosby are quicker off the mark than the Warder and, while his back is turned for the second time, they whip off their disguises. The Warder turns back to look at them again, and is surprised to find himself confronting two entirely different people.

Mullins   Where did they disappear to?

Gilbert   Who?

Mullins   The two men who were here just now. One of them had a ginger beard and the other wore glasses and had a big red nose.

Gilbert   *(indicating the poster)* Like those men there?

Mullins   That's right.

Gilbert   Dunno.

Mullins   How strange. Haven't I seen both your faces, as well, somewhere before?

Gilbert   I shouldn't think so.

Mullins   I have, I'll swear it. I don't suppose either of you are employees of the Gas Board?

Crosby   Yes!

Gilbert   No!

Mullins   Just one tiny moment.

Warder Mullins takes off his false moustache, which somehow enables him to recognise Gilbert and Crosby, who, in turn, recognise the Warder.

It's Gilbert and Crosby!

Gilbert }
Crosby }   Warder Mullins!

> *Gilbert and Crosby run for it, out of the police
> station and across the stage. The Warder blows
> short sharp blasts on his whistle and, after some
> moments, Warder MacBain appears, out of
> breath.*

Mullins   Where've you been?

MacBain   I've had to run down three flights of stairs—if we were
            firemen, you know, we'd have a shiny pole.

Mullins   Come on!

> *The two Warders run out of the police station.
> Gilbert and Crosby meanwhile, in their hysteria,
> have been running hither and thither about the
> stage. As the Warders come out of the station,
> the Convicts again dive into the audience. We
> have another chase around the stalls. At the
> end of the chase, we have again lost both
> Warders and Convicts.*

Scene Two

> *We are back in Detective Constable Grummett's
> house—or a corner of it, at least. Clara Grummett,
> as ordered by her husband, is sitting by the
> telephone, waiting for a call from the kidnappers.
> She is whiling away the time on some domestic
> chore: peeling potatoes, perhaps, or preparing
> sprouts. The telephone rings and she snatches it
> up:*

Clara   Hello? Hello? Is that the black-hearted fiend who took
            away my darling baby? Is that the foul devil who stole
            a mother's pride and joy? Where is he, you evil villain?
            Where is my little darling? If you've harmed one golden
            hair on that innocent head — Hello? *Hello? Who* do
            you want to speak to? . . . I'm afraid there's no one of
            that name here. This is the residence of Detective
            Constable Grummett . . . I think you've dialled the
            wrong number . . . No, there's definitely no one

answering to that name here . . . You've come through
to the stage of the — *(Name of theatre)* — we're in the
middle of a play . . . I'm afraid I can't help you. I can
only suggest that you ring off and dial again. I'm sitting
by the telephone in this play and waiting for it to ring
. . . It's about kidnappers and I'm the distraught
mother, at her wits end, whose only child has been
abducted by kidnappers . . . Yes, my husband would
agree with you, we are living in violent times. Only this
afternoon we had one little boy arrested right out of
our audience and taken to New Scotland Yard . . . He
had a false moustache in his pocket . . . I'm not quite
sure, I think his name was Docherty . . . Kevin Docherty,
I think, but again I'm not quite sure . . . Your name is
Docherty and you have a little boy called Kevin, and you
think he might have been here this afternoon? . . . All I
can suggest, Mr Docherty, is that if your little boy isn't
home by six o'clock, you ring New Scotland Yard . . .
Isn't it 230 1212? . . . Not at all, Mr Docherty, I've
enjoyed talking to you too, but I really must go . . .
Bye-bye.

> *Clara puts down the telephone, sighs, goes back
> to her waiting and her domestic chores. As the
> lights fade on Clara there is a commotion at the
> back of the stalls: short sharp blasts on police
> whistles and cries of "This way!" etc. Gilbert
> and Crosby, still evading their pursuers, make
> their way through the audience and back onto
> the stage again.*

Scene Three

A street, suggested by a wall.

Gilbert   Come on, Cros—we haven't given them the slip yet.

Crosby   It's no use, Gilbert. I'm puffed out. I'll have to have a
            rest.

Gilbert   We can't stop now, man. They're only just behind us.

Crosby   You go on then, I can't. I'm shattered, I am. My knees
            are trembling like two blood donors at a vampires
            tea-party. Look at them. I can't go on. Can't we hide?

Gilbert   Where?

Crosby	Behind this wall.
Gilbert	They're sure to find us there, man! That's the very first place they'll look.
Crosby	They might not.
Gilbert	They will if somebody tells them.
Crosby	Who?
Gilbert	Somebody—anybody. *(Indicating the audience)* Any of these people.
Crosby	They won't give us away. Will you? They'll help us. Won't you?
Gilbert	*(to the audience)* Do you promise? If two gentlemen in warders' uniforms come up here and ask if you've seen two missing convicts go behind this wall, what will you say to them? You couldn't say it a bit louder, could you, a bit more convincingly? That'd be great if you could say it like that!
Crosby	Terrific! They'll believe that all right!
Gilbert	I've just had an idea, Cros!
Crosby	I hope it's better than your other ones.
Gilbert	It's a great idea is this one. It's a bobby-dazzler. We'll disguise ourselves.
Crosby	Not that idea again. You've had that one before. I hate that idea, Gilbert—I do, I really hate that one. We've tried it before and it got us into trouble.
Gilbert	That was when we put on those false noses and beards. But this time it's completely different.
Crosby	How?

Gilbert   We won't put anything *on* this time, we'll take everything off.

Crosby   Take our clothes off?

Gilbert   Yes.

Crosby   Disguise ourselves as nudists, Gilbert?

Gilbert   Not *all* our clothes. Only down to our underwear and our plimmies and socks.

Crosby   What for?

>   *Sounds of shooting and whistles off.*

Gilbert   Look out!

>   *Gilbert and Crosby duck behind the wall. The Warders appear.*

MacBain   It defeats me, they must have vanished into thin air.

Mullins   We'll find them. They must be somewhere. They might have gone behind this wall.

MacBain   Do you think so?

Mullins   I'll ask someone *(To the audience)* Have you seen two missing convicts go by here? They aren't behind this wall, are they, by any chance? Thanks very much. *(To Warder MacBain)* We'll try this way.

>   *The Warders go off. Gilbert and Crosby come out.*

Gilbert   *(to the audience)* That was great. You helped us a lot then.

Crosby   Go on telling me about your idea.

Gilbert   Which idea was that?

Crosby   The one about taking all our clothes off—that idea.

Gilbert   Oh, yes! Well, do you remember that day when the Queen drove past our prison in her big flash car? And all us criminals lined up on the pavement outside and shouted: "Three cheers for Her Royal Majesty!"

Crosby   "Hip-hip-hooray! Hip-hip-hooray!" Yeh! That was a great day, Gilbert! I really enjoyed myself that day. They gave us all little Union Jacks to wave, didn't they? All of us except the murderers.

Gilbert   That's right. What did you do with yours?

>   *Crosby takes a small, crumpled Union Jack from his pocket.*

Crosby   Saved it.

Gilbert does the same.

Gilbert	So did I. And they'll come in useful now. Because when we've stripped off down to our underwear and our plimmies and our socks, we'll stick our Union Jacks on our vests and disguise ourselves as Olympic athletes.
Crosby	I like that idea, Gilbert.
Gilbert	Do you really?
Crosby	Mmmm. *(He nods his head vigorously, then changes it to a shake)* But I don't think it'll work.
Gilbert	Why not?
Crosby	I don't think it would fool Detective Constable Grummett *or* those prison warders. I think they'd see through our disguise.
Gilbert	They won't if everybody helps us again.
Crosby	Helps us how?
Gilbert	*(To the audience)* When I put both of my arms above my head like this—*(He raises his hands above his head like a triumphant sportsman)*—can you all shout: Hooray for the famous Olympic athletes! Let's try it, shall we?
Crosby	That's not bad, Gilbert. But I've got a better idea.
Gilbert	What's that?
Crosby	Supposing we split them down the middle? And all those on that side shout for you, like you said: "Hooray for the famous Olympic athletes!"? And then all these over on this side shout for me, when I put my arms over my head *(He does so)*—like this: "England! England!"
Gilbert	What a great idea! Have you got that, all of you? All this half shout for me: "Hooray for the famous Olympic athletes!" And all you lot over there shout for Convict Crosby: "England! England!" Shall we try it out?
	Crosby and Gilbert ad-lib their shouts with the audience until they are satisfied, then:
	That was fantastic.
Crosby	Terrific. Really great.
Gilbert	That will definitely fool them.
Crosby	And after we've fooled them, Gilbert, what do we do then?
Gilbert	The same as we did before. Make good our escape and then hide again—break into somewhere and lie low.
Crosby	Have we got to?

Gilbert   Of course. We have to keep out of the way until
             Detective Constable Grummett's son is found, or we'll
             get the blame for kidnapping him

Crosby   Hey—I can hear the warders coming back again!

Gilbert   Quick—behind the wall! *(A last word to the audience)*
             Don't forget, will you?

                     *They duck behind the wall. Crosby re-appears
                     and brandishes his fist.*

Crosby   Don't you dare give us away, or you'll get this up your
             hooters.

                     *Gilbert tugs him back behind the wall, just in
                     time, as the two warders re-appear.*

MacBain   It baffles me, it really does, where them two escaped
             hardened criminals can have got to.

Mullins   Well, we're narrowing down the possibilities, aren't we?
             We know they aren't in that direction, because we came
             from there.

MacBain   Correct.

Mullins   And we also know they're not in that direction, either,
             because we've just been there. So, if they're not there
             and they're not there—*(He is pointing off-stage in both
             directions)*—where does that leave?

MacBain   I don't know.

Mullins   It's dead simple! Think! If they're not there and they're
             not there—that only leaves one place they can be.

                     *Warder MacBain looks puzzled, then glances up
                     over his head.*

MacBain   Not up there?

Mullins   No, you great soft stupid nana! They must be *here*!

                     *Warder MacBain looks around, more baffled
                     than before.*

MacBain   But they're not here, are they?

Mullins   How do we know they're not?

MacBain   Because we can't see them.

Mullins   They might be behind that wall.

MacBain   But they're not behind that wall either, are they?

Mullins   How do you know they're not?

MacBain   *(indicating the audience)* Because we asked them, and
             they told us they weren't.

Mullins   How do you know they weren't telling fibs?

MacBain   Them?

Mullins   Yes.

MacBain   Because you've only got to look at their faces to see
           they're not that kind. I mean, the people we had in
           yesterday afternoon—I wasn't surprised that they told
           fibs. But not this lot.

Mullins   I don't know so much. I'm not so sure!

MacBain   Never! They wouldn't tell fibs.

Mullins   Well, I think they would.

MacBain   Oh, no they wouldn't! *(To the audience)* You wouldn't
           tell fibs would you? *(Audience:* No!) There you are,
           you see, what did I tell you? You've only got to look at
           their faces to see that they're honest. *(Back to the
           audience)* And there aren't any escaped convicts hiding
           behind that wall, are there?

Mullins   Are you *sure*? Think very carefully, because it's very
           important *and* very serious. Are there two escaped
           convicts hiding behind that wall?

Audience   No!

MacBain   There you are.

Mullins   Somebody said "yes".

MacBain   Who? I didn't hear anybody.

Mullins   I did. A little boy sitting up there, I distinctly heard him.

MacBain   Well, he's definitely in a very small minority then,
           because all the rest of them shouted "no".

Mullins   I'm going to have a look.

                    *But as he crosses to the wall, Gilbert and
                    Crosby emerge, stripped to their underwear,
                    socks and plimsolls, wearing their Union Jacks
                    on their vests, and striding out with the
                    curious gait of long-distance walkers. They
                    strut round and round the stage, ignoring the
                    warders.*

Mullins   Who the hummers do these two jokers think they are?
                    Warder MacBain shrugs.

MacBain   Don't ask me.

Mullins   Would you say their faces looked at all familiar to you?

MacBain   I'm not sure, now that you come to mention it, there is
           something about them that reminds me of somebody—
           sometime—somewhere . . .

Mullins   Me too—very positively.

              *Gilbert raises his hands above his head and half
              the audience calls out* "Hooray for the famous
              athletes!" *He repeats the gesture, and the cry is
              repeated.*

              Famous Olympic athletes? They don't look very much
              like famous Olympic athletes to me!

MacBain   They might be, you know. That could be where we've
              seen them before—in races on the telly.

Mullins   I doubt it—very much.

              *And, at this point, Crosby raises his arms above
              his head and the other half of the audience calls
              out* "England! England!"

              They're not walking for England, surely?

MacBain   I don't know so much—they might be.

              *And now both Gilbert and Crosby, in turn,
              raise their hands above their heads, and the
              audience yell out both of their chants. Warder
              MacBain gets into the spirit of things, and
              begins to egg on the convicts:*

MacBain   Go on, lads! Come on, England! Get us a gold medal, eh,
              lads?

              *Gilbert and Crosby continue to raise their arms,
              and Warder Mullins too is also caught up in the
              general excitement.*

Mullins   Come on, England! Stick at it! Don't give up!

MacBain   You're well in front, lads! There's no sign of the
              opposition—we're in for a gold *and* a silver! Keep going!

              *And now, as the two convicts raise their hands
              in turn, the warders call out with the audience:*

Warders   Hooray for the famous Olympic athletes! England!
              England!

              *Gilbert and Crosby stride off the stage to
              tumultuous cheering.*

MacBain   Oh, man, wasn't that exciting?

Mullins   It was unbelievable, was that! It really pulled at my
              heart-strings, seeing those lads giving all they've got for
              their country.

MacBain   There was a big lump came into my throat, and I don't
              mind admitting it.

Detective Constable Grummett enters.

Grummett   Hey, hey, hey! What's supposed to be going on?
I thought you two were out after Convicts Gilbert and
Crosby? What are you hanging about here for, yacking?

Mullins   Oh, Detective Constable Grummett, you've just missed
it!

MacBain   It was really grand!

Grummett   What was?

Mullins   We've just seen two Olympic athletes go past.

Grummett   Olympic athletes?

MacBain   Long distance walking lads. They came out from behind
that wall, did a couple of circuits of us, then kicked
their heels and fairly pelted off—they shot away in that
direction.

Mullins   Two England representatives, they were. There's not a
sign as yet of the foreign opposition.

MacBain   We must be racing certainties for the gold *and* the silver
medals.

Grummett   How do you know they were Olympic athletes?

MacBain   They had little Union Jacks on their vests.

Mullins   Like these ones they gave us in the prison. *(He has
pulled a small, crumpled Union Jack from his pocket)*
We all lined up and waved them that day the Queen
drove past.

MacBain   *(also producing his own Union Jack)* That's right, we did.

*A thought strikes the Warders, they stare at
their Union Jacks, horrified.*

Mullins   Hey, wait a minute, you don't think —

MacBain   No, they couldn't have been. They were definitely
Olympic athletes. *(He indicates the audience)* What
about all those people—they were cheering them on as
well.

*Grummett goes behind the wall and returns
carrying the convicts' discarded clothing.*

Grummett   *(disparagingly)* Olympic athletes my detective's identity
card! And who do these prison clothes belong to, do you
reckon then? A couple of international pole-vaulters, I
suppose?

Mullins   Hey—that's Convict Crosby's tie—I'd recognise that
tomato-soup stain anywhere!

MacBain   And that's Convict Gilbert's grubby shirt!

Mullins   They've done the dirty on us yet again!

Grummett   And look here, in this trouser pocket, a ginger beard!
           Does that remind you of anything?

           The Warders look blank and shake their heads.
           Detective Constable Grummett searches the other
           pair of trousers.

Grummett   Then what about these? A pair of glasses and a big
           red conk?

MacBain   Hang on a tick! That rings a bell!

Mullins   It does with me as well. You can't give us a clue, can you,
           Detective Constable Grummett?

Grummett   The kidnappers! Convicts Crosby and Gilbert are not
           only on the run, they're also the pair of rascals
           responsible for the kidnapping of my lad! Get after
           them, you silly stupid men!

                    The two Warders fall over themselves in their
                    haste to follow the convicts. Detective
                    Constable Grummett addresses the audience,
                    severely.

           I bet you thought you were being clever, aiding and
           abetting the escape of two dangerous and habitual
           criminals yet again? I suppose you thought you were
           being funny? I've finished playing games as far as you
           lot are concerned. If you won't play ball with me—very
           well, so be it, I won't play ball with you. I'm taking
           written statements from the lot of you—as of this
           minute. Raise your right hands like this. Come on, don't

mess about. I'm serious. Get your right hands up in the air. Higher! That's a bit more like it. Now then, repeat after me: We swear.

> *Audience:* We swear.

Louder than that. We swear!

> *Audience:* We swear.

To tell the truth to Detective Constable Grummett.
> *Audience:* To tell the truth to Detective Constable Grummett.

And we do hereby promise to tell him the truth, the whole truth, and nothing —

> *Detective Constable Grummett is interrupted in the course of his duty by the arrival of his wife, Clara.*

Clara Stephen, Stephen—whatever do you think you're doing?

Grummett Don't bother me now, Clara—I'm taking a statement from the audience as a whole, and then I have to write it out five hundred times in triplicate and get fifteen hundred signatures.

Clara Statements? Signatures? When our poor unfortunate only child is in the hands of desperate kidnappers?

Grummett All that's in hand as well, my dear. We have their full descriptions.

Clara Of course you have, I gave them to you. They're disguised as bona fide employees of the Gas Board.

Grummett Not any longer, my love. They are now known to have adopted the clothing of Olympic athletes, posing as long-distance walkers representing their country—and yours and mine.

Clara Are you positive, Stephen?

Grummett Absolutely certain. It's been established that they're wearing pants, socks, plimmies and vests with little Union Jacks on them.

Clara What about the ginger beard and the big red conk?

Grummett Both proven false, dearest, and now in my possession. *(He displays them)* Beards and big red conks no longer figure in the case.

Clara And what about the little lad from Row 'J' Kevin Docherty, with the false moustache, who got taken in for questioning?

Grummett What about him?

Clara   I was just wondering, that's all. I was speaking to his
            father on the telephone. He sounded ever such a nice
            man. He was very worried about Kevin. That's why I
            came looking for you. I thought you ought to know.

Grummett   Did you get a phone call from the kidnappers?

Clara   I'm afraid not, dearest. Only Mr Docherty. No, I tell a
            lie. A man rang up for a Takeaway Chinese Christmas
            dinner—wrong number. Oh, yes! And Mr Allardyce
            phoned.

Grummett   Allardyce? Allardyce?

Clara   You know Mr Allardyce. Alexander's headmaster. He
            rang to wish us a Merry Christmas. I told him about the
            kidnapping and he proffered us his deepest sympathy.
            Wasn't that kind?

Grummett   Very.

Clara   Oh, yes! Something else you'll be pleased to hear. Our
            Alexander's been made hamster monitor in his class next
            year.

Grummett   What's a hamster monitor?

Clara   He feeds the hamster, dearest. So if Alexander isn't
            rescued before the start of next term, we're to let Mr
            Allardyce know, so our little furry friends won't
            starve.

Grummett   Hamsters! Takeaway Chinese Christmas dinners! You
            were supposed to be taking phone calls from kidnappers
            —not getting involved with headmasters and Chinese
            restaurants and parents of children in the audience.

Clara   Yes, and you're a fine one to talk, Stephen Grummett,
            standing here writing down five hundred statements
            instead of tracking down the desperadoes who have
            abducted little Alexander, the apple of his mother's
            eye.

Grummett   I'm on their trail, Clara. I've men out now. They won't
            escape me much longer, now that I know their true
            identities.

Clara   Who are they?

Grummett   Your two so-called bona fide employees of the Gas
            Board, alias my two Olympic athletes, are really a couple
            of escaped convicts, habitual criminals by the names of
            Gilbert and Crosby. Old enemies of mine.

Clara   Oh, horror upon horrors! My own darlingest boy in the clutches of escaped convicts and habitual criminals! Go after them, Stephen! Hurry! Travel like the wind before it is too late! Hunt them down like the wild animals they really are!

Grummett *(with a sigh)* Very well, dear. But you go home where you belong, and wait for me—*please*.

Clara   Whatever you think best.

> *Grummett puts his notebook away, moves to leave, then pauses to glower at the audience and say:*

Grummett But don't think you're going to get away scot free—because I haven't finished with you lot, yet, not by a long chalk.

> *Grummett goes off.*

Clara   Go home and wait, he says! How can I wait, when my own dearest darling precious angel is in the hands of desperate men who will stop at nothing?

> *Clara is addressed from the back of the stalls by Mrs Evadne Docherty, a lady with an umbrella and shopping basket.*

Evadne   Excuse me! I say, excuse me, love!

Clara   Yes, what is it?

> *Evadne Docherty makes her way to the front of the stalls.*

Evadne   Excuse me for interrupting you, but aren't you the lady my hubby was talking to not long ago?

Clara   I don't think so, dear.

Evadne   I think you'll find you are, love, according to this programme. Aren't you Detective Constable Grummett's wife?

Clara   That's right.

Evadne   Then you *are* the lady I'm looking for. I'm Mrs Docherty.

Clara   Mrs Docherty?

Evadne   Little Kevin's mummy. The little boy from Row 'J' who was taken in for questioning. You passed words with my hubby on the telephone.

Clara   Oh, *that* Mrs Docherty. Come up on the stage.

Evadne   Am I allowed?

Clara   Well, not normally, no—but considering the circumstances. It's funny you turning up like this, I was only speaking to my hubby about your hubby not two minutes ago. Is there any news of Kevin?

Evadne   *(having made her way onto the stage)* Well, no—it's very worrying.

Clara   You have my sympathy, Mrs Docherty. I know exactly how you feel.

Evadne   Oooh, yes! My hubby told me—you've had your little cherub kidnapped in the play, haven't you?

                     Clara nods her head, sadly.

             And isn't there any news of him?

Clara   Only that he's been adbucted by two hardened criminals, escaped convicts.

Evadne   How dreadful for you! I shouldn't have come here, should I? Bothering you with my problems.

Clara   That's quite all right—it's nice to have someone to talk to.

Evadne   Well, I know! My hubby said to me, before he set off for Scotland Yard, "Don't go out of the house," he said, "in case anyone should telephone."

Clara   That's exactly what Stephen, my hubby, said to me. But you can't just sit there on your own.

Evadne   You can't, you can't! "I'll slip my coat on," I said to myself, "and I'll go down to that theatre. It might not do any good," I said. "But it's better than sitting here worrying, not knowing what's happening."

Clara   You did the best thing too.

Evadne   What are you going to do?

Clara   Go after my hubby, Detective Constable Grummett, who's gone in search of his men, who have gone in search of the kidnappers.

Evadne   Would you mind very much if I come with you?

Clara   Not at all, Mrs Docherty, I'd like you to.

Evadne   You're sure I won't get in the way of the plot?

Clara   Of course you won't. I'd appreciate it. I never did like being on my own in a play—you never know who you might come across next. It's not like real life, you know. You can come up against all sorts of terrors on a stage. Murderers, vampires, foreign agents, horrible hairy spiders. Do you know I once walked onto a stage and there was this great big two-headed giant!

Evadne   Never!

Clara   There was! In Jack and the Beanstalk, at the Palace
            Theatre, Westcliff-on-Sea. I was only young, I played a
            Singing Harp. It's branded on my memory. Come on
            then, this way. But do watch out—you can meet all
            kinds of monsters in a theatre!

            *They go off, in some trepidation. Their fears
            are not entirely without foundation, for,
            following them across the stage comes
            Frankenstein's Monster. His green head and
            bolted neck are slightly offset by the fact that
            he is wearing a mackintosh, bowler hat, and is
            carrying a briefcase. The Monster hurries off as,
            with him, we hear police whistles in the
            auditorium. The two Warders pursue Gilbert and
            and Crosby around the stalls while a scene
            change is effected and the lights go up on:*

Scene Four

            *A spooky green cellar, reminiscent of
            Frankenstein's subterranean laboratory. There
            are three entrances: a heavy oak door at the
            back: a dark and creepy archway on one side
            and, on the other side, a dank and ghastly
            passage. We hear the sound of rusty bolts
            being drawn and the oak door creaks open.
            Frankenstein's Monster enters. He takes off
            his mackintosh and his bowler hat and hangs
            them up on a row of pegs which already
            contain various items of clothing: white linen
            overalls and trousers etc. The Monster crosses
            and throws an enormous switch on the wall
            which sets off a blinding flash of electricity.
            The Monster, apparently satisfied, goes off
            through the archway. The oak door opens
            again, slowly, and Gilbert and Crosby peer
            inside. They are still dressed in their
            underclothing.*

Crosby   What's this place, Gilbert?
Gilbert   I don't know. But at least we haven't made the same

mistake as last time—it definitely isn't Detective Constable Grummett's living room. We'll be safe down here.

Crosby	It's a bit spooky.
Gilbert	Stop moaning, Crosby. You're always *moaning*.
Crosby	Well—I don't like spooky places, Gilbert. Especially spooky cellars. I hate spooky cellars, I really *hate* them. I wish I was back in my nice warm cell.
Gilbert	We've lost Detective Constable Grummett, haven't we? And we've given the slip to those two warders. So what is there to be afraid of?
Crosby	What's through that dark and creepy archway?
Gilbert	I don't know. Nothing to be afraid of.
Crosby	*(indicating the passage)* And what about that dank and ghastly passage?
Gilbert	There's nothing there either.
Crosby	You're just saying that.
Gilbert	No, I'm not.
Crosby	Yes, you are! You baffle me sometimes! The things you say. That passage looks to me as if it's stuffed with bats and rats and horrible hairy spiders' webbies.
Gilbert	Come and look then.
Crosby	I should cocoa!

Gilbert   All right, stay here. I'm going.

> *Gilbert sets off along the dank and ghastly passage. Crosby, left alone, glances around and trembles.*

Crosby   Wait for me, Gilbert!

> *Crosby follows Gilbert. A moment later, the Monster comes out of the dark and creepy archway, carrying a sinister parcel. He goes out through the oak door which creaks shut behind him, and we hear the rusty bolts closing. Crosby and Gilbert return.*

Gilbert   What did I tell you? There's nothing down there but actors' dressing rooms and old scenery—there's nothing to be afraid of.

Crosby   But I *heard* something.

Gilbert   You imagined it.

Crosby   No, I didn't—I definitely heard this noise—these noises— like a door creaking, then rusty bolts shutting.

Gilbert   You couldn't have done. There's nobody here but us.

Crosby   You don't know what might be down that dark and creepy archway. It looks to me as if it's crammed with bloodstained headless ghouls and grinning chained-up skelegogs.

Gilbert   Let's go and look.

Crosby   Not me, mate! I've had enough of this place. I know
           when I'm well off—I'm going back to prison.

Gilbert   Please yourself, Crosby. I'm going through that archway.

> *Gilbert goes through the dark and creepy
> archway.*

Crosby   He's raving bonkers! He wants his head examining! I
           wouldn't stay in this place if you paid me!

> *Crosby goes to the door, finds it bolted on the
> outside, tugs at it and panics.*

Help! Help! We've been locked in! We're entombed!
Incarcerated! Help! *(He pauses in his struggle to open
the door, glances around, and is beset by fears of his
surroundings)* Gilbert! . . . Gilbert!

> *Crosby scurries off through the dark and
> creepy archway. We hear the bolts being
> withdrawn, and the Monster re-enters. He
> closes the oak door and goes off down the
> dank and ghastly passage. Crosby and
> Gilbert return.*

Don't say I didn't tell you so, Gilbert, because I did.
But it's always the same with you, you always know best,
you just won't listen!

Gilbert   I don't know what you're worrying about, Crosby.
           There's nothing to be afraid of.

Crosby   Nothing to be afraid of!

Gilbert   No, there's nothing through that dark and creepy
           archway except the men who change the scenery and
           the lady that works the curtains.

Crosby   Oh, no, there's nothing to be afraid of, mate, nothing at
          all! Entombed in a spooky green cellar with a dark and
          creepy archway and a dank and ghastly passage! That's
          all! Flippin' well incarcerated, Gilbert! But, oh no,
          there's nothing to be afraid of, is there!

Gilbert   Locked in where? How?

Crosby   In here! That's how! You try that door, matey, you'll
          soon see whether we're locked in or not!

Gilbert   *(tries the door)* It's open.

Crosby   Is it?

Gilbert   Of course it is—look!

Crosby   It was locked a minute ago.

Gilbert   It wasn't locked. It's never been locked, you imagined it.

Crosby   Don't say that. I am not in the habit of imagining things,
          Gilbert. Well—I admit I *do* imagine some things,
          occasionally. Like blood-stained headless ghouls and
          chained-up grinning skelegogs—all like that.

Gilbert   And what about bats and rats and horrible hairy spiders'
          webbies?

Crosby   Yes, them too, occasionally. But I do not imagine doors
          being locked when they're open, matey. Oh, no! I *tried*
          that door, Gilbert, with both hands. And it was locked,
          most definitely. And when you try things with both hands
          hands that's not imagining. *(To the audience)* Is it?
          *(Audience: No! An idea occurs to Crosby, and again he
          speaks to the audience)* Hey, did you see me when I
          tried to open this door? (*Audience:* Yes!) And it was
          locked, wasn't it? (*Audience:* Yes!) There you are!

Gilbert   It wasn't locked, was it? (*Audience:* Yes!) Are you sure?
          (*Audience:* Yes!) It wasn't! (*Audience:* It was!) Oh, no
          it wasn't!

Crosby   Hey, you didn't by any remote chance happen to spot
          who it was that locked it, did you? (*Audience:* Yes!)
          Who was it? (*Audience:* Frankenstein's Monster!) Who?
          (*Audience:* Frankenstein's Monster) Flippin' holy
          Moses, it wasn't was it? Did you hear that, Gilbert? We
          were locked in this cellar by Frankenstein's Monster!

Gilbert   You're not going to swallow that, are you, Crosby?
          They're pulling your leg.

Crosby   I don't care! I believe them! Come on, Gilbert, let's get
          on our bikes, let's get out of it!

Gilbert	*(to the audience)* If it was Frankenstein's Monster, where did it go to? *(The audience yell and point down the dank and ghastly passage. Gilbert mistakes their meaning, and looks in the opposite direction)* What? Through that dark and creepy archway?
	Cries of No! from the audience.
Crosby	Down the dank and ghastly passage? *(Audience: Yes!)* Come on, Gilbert, let's go now while the going's good!
Gilbert	I've told you, Crosby, they're having you on. They don't have Frankenstein's Monsters in Christmas plays, man!
Crosby	They don't have spooky green cellars either, but they've got one in this!
Gilbert	Come with me.
Crosby	Where to?
Gilbert	Through there. Down the passage.
Crosby	I'm not going down there again! What for? To come face to face with Frankenstein's Monster in a dank and ghastly passage, full of bats and rats and horrible hairy spiders' webbies! Do you think I'm barmy or something?
Gilbert	I'll prove to you that there's no monster. Now, come on!
	Gilbert steps warily into the dank and ghastly passage. Crosby, with some hesitation, follows him. Frankenstein's Monster comes out of the dark and creepy archway. He is carrying another sinister parcel. He pulls down the wall switch, there is another flash, and he goes out through the oak door. Again we hear the rusty bolts squeak home. Gilbert and Crosby return.
Gilbert	Now do you believe me? There's no Frankenstein's Monster, is there?
Crosby	No, Gilbert.
Gilbert	Frankenstein's Monster, in a Christmas play? I've never heard of anything so ridiculous in all my life! You might as well have the Big Bad Wolf in Cinderella! *(To the audience)* And you lot ought to be ashamed of yourselves, trying to frighten escaped convicts—as if they hadn't got enough to worry about. Why did you say there was a monster? *(Audience: There is!)* There isn't!! *(Audience: There is!)* No there isn't, we've been right along that dank and ghastly passage, there's not even a little tidgy monster, let alone a Frankenstein one.

(Audience: He came out of there!—*or words to that effect)* He what, you say? Came out of where? There? Out of the dark and creepy archway? (*Audience:* Yes!) But you said he went up the dank and ghastly passage? How could he go up the dank and ghastly passage and then come out of the dark and creepy archway? It's not possible.

Crosby   *(has discovered the door is locked again)* Oh, crikey, Gilbert, it's happened again.

Gilbert   What's the matter now?

Crosby   It's locked us in! We're entombed once more—incarcerated!

Gilbert   Stand back out of the way, Crosby. It's just got stuck or something. *(He tries the door)* Hey up, man—you're right! It is locked! I wonder who did that then? *(To the audience)* Who did you say? (*Audience:* Frankenstein's Monster!*)* Do you want to know what I think, Cros? I don't think they have been kidding us—we *have* been locked in down here by Frankenstein's Monster.

Crosby   I knew it! I knew it all along! *(He begins to shake and his knees start to knock)* Oh, crikey! This is the last time I escape from prison with you, Gilbert!

Gilbert   Don't panic, lad. Don't let it get you down. Just look at the way you're trembling. You've got to try and look on the bright side.

Crosby   Don't panic? Look on what bright side? We've been locked inside a spooky green cellar by a monster, and you you have the cheek to say 'Don't let it get you down!' But I'll tell you why I'm trembling, Gilbert—not because I'm frightened—well, not *just* because I'm frightened—as well as that, I'm shivering because I'm stood here in my underwear.

Gilbert   You're right. It is a bit parky.

        Gilbert looks around and sees the clothing hanging on the pegs.

Gilbert   We might not be able to get out of here, but we can do something about being cold though. We can put these clothes on.

        Gilbert gives Crosby a white overall and a pair of white linen trousers, and takes the same for himself.

Crosby   What sort of clothes are these? Whose are they?

Gilbert   Does it matter? Just so long as they keep out the cold.

Crosby   Of course it matters, man! You know what these are,
            don't you? White clothes—these are doctor's clothes.
            They belong to Doctor Frankenstein, I shouldn't
            wonder!

Gilbert   Get them on, Cros, stop grumbling.

Crosby   *(also getting dressed, but not without protest)* You're
            too quick at pinching other people's belongings,
            Gilbert! You nicked Detective Constable Grummett's
            crisps and sweeties, didn't you? And where did that get
            us? Into bother. And now you've got us pinching
            Doctor Frankenstein's overalls and trousers—I suppose
            you think he'll thank us for it!

Gilbert   *(is now wearing the white clothing, and is somewhat
            perturbed)* Crosby?

Crosby   What is it?

Gilbert   I've just had a terrible thought.

Crosby   What is it?

Gilbert   I think I *know* where we are!

Crosby   Is that all? I can tell you where we are, man. Have you
            only just realised? We're in Doctor Frankenstein's
            laboratory. And he's going to stroll in at any moment
            and catch us in his trousers!

Gilbert   No, we're not, Cros! I only wish we were! If we're where
            I think we are, we're in a much more horrible place than
            that.

Crosby   Where's that, Gilbert?

Gilbert   I want to be sure first—just look around and see if you
            can see a big switch anywhere?

            *They both search the walls, Crosby discovers
            the switch that was thrown by Frankenstein's
            Monster.*

Crosby   Is this it?

Gilbert   That's definitely it, all right—that definitely proves it!

Crosby   What? Doesn't that prove we're in Doctor
            Frankenstein's laboratory then? Isn't that the switch he
            switches on for electrifying monsters?

Gilbert   I've already told you, Cros, we're in a far, far worse
            place than that, old lad. We're in one of the most terrible
            places that was ever invented by man or beast.

Crosby   Where are we, Gilbert—tell me?

Gilbert   We're in an underground school dinner factory!

Crosby   We're not, are we?

Gilbert   Most definitely. Look at the clothes we're wearing—not
          doctors' clothes, Cros—cooks' clothes. And look at that
          switch—that's the switch they switch on for starting the
          machinery that puts the lumps in mashed potatoes. They
          put the lumps in here and pack them off to unsuspecting
          boys and girls throughout the country.

Crosby   What about the lumpy custard?

Gilbert   That as well. They'll put lumps in anything: taties,
          custard, gravy—even bread pudding. You name it, this is
          where they stick the lumps in. And take a deep smell,
          Crosby, can't you niff something really awful?

Crosby   *(takes a deep sniff)* It does pong a bit off, now that
          you come to mention it. Sort of bad eggs and rotten
          cabbage.

Gilbert   School dinners.

Crosby   But what was Frankenstein's Monster doing in a school
          dinner factory?

Gilbert   I don't know, and I don't intend to stay here long
          enough to find out.

Crosby   I don't know what you *do* intend to do then, Gilbert—
          because in case it's slipped your memory, kiddo—we're
          entombed. Incarcerated. *(He shudders)* I hate school
          dinners, Gilbert—I do, I really hate them.

Gilbert   I'm going to have another good scout round, up that
          passage and through that archway—there could still be
          another way out of here.

Crosby   I'll come with you.

Gilbert   You won't. You'll hang on here, in case that Monster
          returns. If it does, get your back up against that door.

Crosby   Give over, man! You're not suggesting I can hold a
          door shut, are you, with Frankenstein's Monster huffing
          and puffing on the other side? *(But Gilbert has already
          gone up the dank and ghastly passage)* Gilbert? Hey,
          kid,—come back here a little minute! Gil—bert! Do you
          want a piece of choco-lert! Gilly-Gilly-Gillo!

                    *As Crosby calls up the dank and ghastly
                    passage, Gilbert appears out of the dark and
                    creepy archway. He tiptoes across and:*

Gilbert   Booo!

Crosby   *(jumps in the air)* Show some sense, man—you could give
             somebody a heart attack doing that! Where did you
             spring from?

Gilbert   Through there. The same way that Frankenstein's
             Monster went. It's easy. You just walk round the back
             of the scenery. I'll tell you something else—there's a
             little door round the back that's bolted from the
             outside. I'm going back to have a look inside it.

Crosby   Hang on a tick, don't be rotten —

             *But again Gilbert has gone, this time through
             the dark and creepy archway. Crosby peers up
             the archway, then, on second thoughts, crosses
             to peer up the dank and ghastly tunnel. But
             Gilbert does return through the archway, his
             hands held high above his head, backing away
             from Alexander Grummett. Alexander, once
             again, is pointing a gun at Gilbert.*

Alexander   Stick 'em up!

Crosby   *(without turning round)* Oh no, I'm not falling for
             another trick, Gilbert, so don't try it a second time!

             *Alexander pulls the trigger and a shot rings out,
             dislodging a stone cornice or a cellar gargoyle.
             Crosby again jumps in the air, and turns round.*

Crosby   Oh no! Not him again!

Gilbert   I'm afraid so, Cros—and it's not a water pistol this time.

Alexander   Hands up, or else I'll blast you into smithereens—
             Kerpow! Kerpow!

Crosby   *(raising his hands)* What's he doing here?

Gilbert   He was locked inside that little door.

Alexander   Where you two baddies put me, when you kidnapped me.
             But you didn't know you dropped this gun in there when
             you locked me in, did you?

Crosby   We didn't lock you in there!

Alexander   Quiet—or you'll get it now: Kerboom! Kerboom!
             Kerpow! I thought "Right," I thought, "Rightyho, I'll
             get them two when they come back!" And I have got
             you, haven't I? Ker*poo!* Ker*poo! Kersplatt!* You wait
             till my dad gets here, he'll murder you with one hand
             tied behind his back. He'll spifflicate you blindfolded.

Gilbert	It wasn't us, kid, honest. We're locked in the same as you. You try that door.
Alexander	Don't try any of your tricks again.
Crosby	It's true! We are locked in. In an underground school dinner factory. All three of us. And it wasn't me and Gilbert that kidnapped you. It was Frankenstein's Monster.
Alexander	There's no such thing as Frankenstein's Monster. He's only in old films on the telly.
Gilbert	There is! We've seen him! Well, not us, exactly. But *they* have. Look—I'll prove it to you. *(To the audience)* Did we lock this little lad in that cupboard? (*Audience:* No!) Was it Frankenstein's Monster? (*Audience:* Yes!) Now will you believe us?
Alexander	On your baddies' oath?
Gilbert ⎱ Crosby ⎰	On our baddies' oath.

> *They draw their forefingers across their throats and spit.*

Gilbert	It was Frankenstein's Monster, honest to God, and we'll have to be quick—he'll be back any minute.
Alexander	I've always wanted to get a monster! I'll hide in that archway. As soon as he walks in the door I'll splatt him right between the eyes: Ker*pow!* Ker*splatt!* Ker*pow!*
Gilbert	That's no good. You can't get Frankenstein's Monster with a gun. The bullets go straight through him—he doesn't even feel them, sonny.
Crosby	Crikey Moses, that's true!
Gilbert	But we might be able to frighten him away, though, when he comes in. And if he runs off and forgets to lock the door, we could get away ourselves.
Crosby	Frighten away a monster? Us?
Gilbert	Why not? Everybody's afraid of something. If we could only find out what puts the wind up Frankenstein's Monster we'd be laughing.
Crosby	He's not supposed to be all that fond of Dracula, is he?
Alexander	Or werewolves.
Gilbert	Dracula and werewolves, that's it!
Crosby	Only I haven't got any fangs, Gilbert, and I don't see you sprouting a tail within the next few minutes.

Gilbert   We don't have to *look* like them, as long as we *sound* like them. It's quite dark down here, he might not notice.

Crosby   We couldn't make enough noise, just the three of us.

Gilbert   Not on our own, no. But with a bit of help . . . *(To the audience)* Will you? *(Audience:* Yes!) Half of you be Draculas, that's you lot over here. And when I give the signal, like this, you must all stick your fingers in the air and go: "Wheeee!" Do you think you can do that? Shall we try it? *(Audience:* Wheeee!) Great! Fantastic!!

Crosby   And the rest of you be werewolves. That's all you ones over here. And when I give the signal, put your hands to your mouths and all go: "Whooo!" Have a go, eh? *(Audience:* Whoooo!) That's terrific.

Gilbert   Now let's have a proper rehearsal. We'll let young Master Grummett pretend to be Frankenstein's Monster. I'll hide in the dark and creepy archway, and Crosby, you get in the dank and ghastly passage. *(To Alexander)* And you go to the door and pretend to be Frankenstein's Monster coming in. Okay?

> *Gilbert and Crosby take up their positions. Alexander turns at the door and staggers in. Gilbert signals from the archway, and half the audience go "Wheeee!" then Crosby signals from the passage and the other half go "Whoooo!" Alexander simulates fear and turns and runs. They ad-lib another rehearsal.*

Gilbert   That's really great—that frightened me, did that, and I knew who it was. I should think it'll terrify the monster.

Crosby   Gilbert—quick! I can hear it coming!

Gilbert   *(to Alexander)* You come with me.

> *The three of them hide. We hear the bolts being drawn from outside. The door creaks open, slowly, and Frankenstein's Monster enters. He crosses into the cellar towards the audience. Gilbert signals. Half the audience goes "Wheeee!" Crosby signals. The other half of the audience goes "Whoooo!" Frankenstein's Monster takes off his head—which is a mask— and reveals the stern features of Headmaster Horace Winston Allardyce.*

Allardyce   *(to the audience)* Disgraceful behaviour! *(He glances into the passage and the archway)* Come out of there at once! Whoever you are!

> *Gilbert, Crosby and Alexander come out, sheepishly. Alexander tries to hide behind Gilbert.*

Allardyce   Who are you? And what are you doing here?

Gilbert   We were going to ask you the same question.

Allardyce   *(peering at Alexander)* Isn't that young Grummett? from Mr Gilhooley's class?

Alexander   Yes, sir.

Allardyce   Don't mumble, lad! And stand up straight! Don't slouch! And kindly address me by my proper title! Now, speak up—are you or are you not Alexander Grummett?

Alexander   Yes, Headmaster.

Gilbert   Headmaster?

Crosby   Aren't you Frankenstein's Monster then?

Allardyce   Do I *look* like Frankenstein's Monster? Get your shoulders back, Grummett! And don't pick your nose! *(Alexander mumbles back at him)* Speak up, boy!

Alexander   I wasn't picking my nose, Headmaster. I was scratching it.

Allardyce   Then don't. *(Back to Crosby)* I am Horace Winston Allardyce, Headmaster of South End Lane North Comprehensive School, as this wretch, who happens to be one of my pupils, can testify. *(To the audience)* As for you lot. Your behaviour leaves a great deal to be desired! I shall deal most severely with the next child that makes a disgusting noise. And you grown-ups ought to know better than to allow children to behave in that disgusting fashion! Sit up straight. Pay attention! Hands on heads—arms folded—hands on heads! Better. I am watching very carefully a small boy, sitting up there, who hasn't moved a muscle yet. You'll all be waiting outside my office tomorrow morning if you don't buck your ideas up! Hands on heads! Arms folded! Much better. *(Back to Gilbert and Crosby)* Who are you?

Crosby   We're Gilbert and Crosby. I'm Crosby and he's Gilbert.

Allardyce   And who might Gilbert and Crosby be, pray? And what are they doing trespassing in the School Dinner Factory?

Crosby   We're . . . We're . . .

Gilbert   We're just a couple of fellows—ships cooks who lost our

	way and stumbled in this cellar. But if you *aren't* Frankenstein's Monster, why are you dressed up like him? And what are you doing in a School Dinner Factory on Christmas Eve?
Allardyce	*(With a glance at his Frankenstein costume)* I am on my way to the Headmasters' Christmas Eve Fancy Dress Ball, if it's any business of yours. An annual event attended by headmasters from all over England. We like to let our hair down once a year. As to your second question, I called in here this evening to do a favour for a very good friend of mine. The Governor of North End Lane South Maximum Security Prison.
Crosby	Not Governor Martindale?
Allardyce	Yes, do you know him?
Gilbert	No.
Crosby	Nor me either—I've never even heard of him.
Allardyce	It seems they've run out of lumpy potatoes for the convicts' Christmas Dinner tomorrow. I said I'd call in here on my way to the Fancy Dress Ball and pick some up. I have them outside in my car, if you care to look.
Gilbert	And it wasn't you that kidnapped young Grummett then?
Allardyce	Kidnapped Grummett? *Is* he kidnapped? Now that you come to mention it, his mother did say something on the phone. Are you kidnapped, Grummett?
Alexander	Yes, Headmaster.
Allardyce	Will you speak up, boy! You're in your third year of elocution study and I cannot understand one word you say! Are you or are you not kidnapped?
Alexander	Yes, Headmaster.
Allardyce	Then believe me, gentlemen, I was not the one. Were it my wish to kidnap anyone—which it isn't—I should choose a more salubrious victim than Master Grummett, believe you me! Don't scratch, lad—and put your pullover straight!
Gilbert	But if *you* didn't kidnap him –
Crosby	And we didn't kidnap him –
Gilbert	Who did?

At which point, Detective Constable Grummett steps into the cellar.

Grummett   Alexander, thank God you're safe! I've combed the country! Gilbert and Crosby, caught red-handed, I'll see you pay for this! You villainous kidnappers! Give me that gun, son, I'll keep them covered.

Allardyce   Is it Mr Grummett, Alexander's father?

Grummett   Hello, Headmaster! Detective Constable Grummett, actually —

Allardyce   Yes, I thought it was. Where've you been hiding yourself, Mr Grummett?

Grummett   Nowhere.

Allardyce   Well, you certainly haven't put in an appearance at any of our Parent Teacher Association meetings over the last six months.

Grummett   I've been rather tied up, Headmaster, at New Scotland Yard —

Allardyce   Neither were you at our Speech Day.

Grummett   I think I was busy arresting someone that afternoon —

Allardyce   Or the School Sports, *or* the Nativity Play last week. Were you in the Nativity Play, Grummett?

Alexander   Yes, Headmaster

Allardyce   Diction, lad! Voice! Speak up!

Alexander   Yes, Headmaster. I was a shepherd.

Grummett   I was sorry to have to miss that, Headmaster. Give us the gun, Alexander, before these villains make a run for it.

Allardyce   All in good time, Mr Grummett. When I've said my piece You see, we put on these extra-mural activities in school, particularly for the parents' benefits. A great many of the school staff work jolly hard, Mr Grummett, and it's a jolly bad show—at least, I think it is—when parents don't even bother to show up. A jolly bad show indeed!

Grummett I'm definitely down for the Spring Gymnastic Display, Headmaster, most definitely. Give us the gun, son —

Allardyce I hope so, Mr Grummett. You see, if you don't co-operate with us, we can hardly give of our best, as teachers. And then parents wonder why children get kidnapped and mumble under their breath instead of speaking up.

Grummett I know, Headmaster but as far as the Spring Gymnastic Display goes, I think you'll find the wife, Mrs Grummett, is turning up as well—that'll make two of us. Give us the gun, lad! Quick!

Gilbert Hang on! Where's your gun, Detective Constable Grummett?

Grummett None of your business, Convict Gilbert.

Gilbert I think it is. *(He snatches the gun from Alexander)* And I'll take this.

Grummett Now, don't try anything, Gilbert. You'll give me that gun, if you know what's good for you. You're in enough hot water as things stand!

Gilbert Not as much as you, Detective Constable Grummett— because this *is* your gun!

Crosby It's what, Gilbert?

Gilbert This is Detective Constable Grummett's police gun. It's got his name on it. Stephen Grummett, D.C., C.I.D. So you tell us, Detective Constable Grummett, what your gun was doing in that locked room with the little lad? Because as far as I can see, it means you kidnapped your own son.

Grummett What absolute utter tripe, rubbish and total balderdash! Whoever heard of anyone kidnapping his own son!

> *Grummett makes a move towards Crosby and Gilbert, but Gilbert keeps him at bay with the gun.*

Gilbert Get back!

Grummett Warder Mullins! Warder MacBain!

> *The two Warders burst into the room, both carrying guns.*

Grummett Seize those escaped convicts and kidnappers—disarm them!

Allardyce MacBain? Did you say MacBain? It isn't Trevor MacBain, is it?

MacBain   It is, Headmaster.

Allardyce   Yes, I thought it might be! I'll be blowed! I took you for History and Trigonometry in 1968, didn't I? Wasn't it you I once caught smoking in the boiler room?

MacBain   Yes, Headmaster.

Allardyce   Yes, I thought I did. Just hold your horses, MacBain. And you—whatever your name is.

Mullins   It's Mullins, Headmaster. Billy Mullins.

Allardyce   Billy Mullins! Is it really? How time does fly! Form 3A, 1962! *(Mullins nods)* You set the cricket pavilion on fire! *(Mullins hangs his head in shame)* You stand over there, Mullins. Do as *I* say. Now, Grummett, I'm not satisfied with your explanation either! What about that gun?

   At which point, Clara Grummett and Evadne Docherty enter.

Clara   No, and neither am I, Stephen Grummett! Alexander, my baby boy, my only darling, come to mummy's arms! *(Alexander flings himself into his mother's arms)* Hello, Headmaster! I've been listening outside with this nice lady.

Allardyce   It's Mrs Docherty, is it not? This is a surprise. How's little Kevin enjoying his holidays?

Evadne   Not very much, Headmaster. He's been taken in for questioning to New Scotland Yard, by this kind lady's husband.

Allardyce   Kevin Docherty? I can't believe it! He's one of the brightest and best-mannered lads in his class—in the whole school if it comes to that! Whatever for?

Evadne   Well may you ask, Headmaster! Because I'm sure I don't know. And it comes to something if a little tot can't go to a theatre in safety any longer. Why, I used to go everywhere when I was a child—by myself—Puss-in-Boots at the old Empire that's been pulled down. Babes in the Wood at the Royalty, the one that they turned into a supermarket. I've never ever heard of anybody being arrested at a Christmas play before!

Allardyce   No, and neither have I. I think you've got some explaining to do, Detective Constable Grummett.

Grummett   All right. It's a fair cop. It was me that did it. I kidnapped our Alexander *and* got the Docherty kid taken in for questioning. I did that to put the other detectives off the scent.

Evadne   An innocent child!

Clara   *Two* innocent children—one his own flesh and blood.

Evadne   I think you ought to be deeply ashamed!

Grummett   I am, Mrs Docherty, I truly am.

Clara   Your own *son*. You kidnapped him. What *for*? Why, Stephen, *why*? Tell us, in the name of heaven.

Grummett   I'm sorry, Clara. It was tomorrow morning that was on my mind.

Clara   Christmas morning?

Grummett   When he woke up and looked in his stocking. All those things he'd asked for. An air rifle. A pop-gun. A new water-pistol. A ping-pong ball bazooka. A ballistic missile. A jet-propelled target seeking rocket. And he'd be dashing dashing round the house like every morning, only worse. Kerboom, kerboom! Kersplatt! Kerpow! Kerpoo, kerpoo! All like that. Driving me mad. It was no use, Clara, I knew that my nerves just wouldn't stand it. And then something snapped inside my head.

Clara   I only hope Somebody up there can see His way to forgiving you, Stephen Grummett—because I know I never shall.

Grummett   It was only for the *one* day, Clara, love. I swear it. I'd have let him out for Boxing Day. I just wanted a bit of peace on one Christmas morning—I mean, after all—isn't that what Christmas is supposed to be all about? Peace?

Allardyce   You'll get your peace where you're going, Detective Constable Grummett. All the peace you want. Take him away, Warder Mullins.

Warder Mullins puts his hand on Detective

Constable Grummett's shoulder and leads him away.

Gilbert   I suppose we'll have to go back and serve our time as well, Cros?

Crosby   It looks very much like it, Gilbert.

Gilbert   Here's Detective Constable Grummett's gun, Mrs Grummett. No doubt he'll want it back again, when he's paid his debt to society.

Allardyce   Goodbye, Gilbert. Goodbye, Crosby. I'll say this much for you both: you might be desperate hardened escaped convicts who will stop at nothing—but you're not bad lads at heart. Merry Christmas to the pair of you.

Gilbert and Crosby manage to give Allardyce a wan smile as they are led away.

MacBain   Come on.

Crosby   *(as they go)* I say, Warder MacBain? You don't happen to know, I don't suppose, by any chance, whether or not we're having crackers with our Christmas prison dinners tomorrow?

Allardyce   Well, ladies, I'm pleased that you two have got to know each other, if nothing else good has come of this affair.

Clara   It's the only nice thing that's happened all evening, Headmaster.

Evadne   We seemed to hit it off together very well, right from the time we said 'hello'.

Allardyce   We're looking for two bright sparks tonight, at the Headmasters' Christmas Eve Fancy Dress Ball—to run the raffle and judge the Fancy Dress Competition. There's a grammar school headmaster from Darlington who's coming as a pillar-box. It'll take your minds off unhappier events. Do you think you'd both be interested?

Clara   I shall have to take Alexander home first, Headmaster, but afterwards . . .

Evadne   And I shall have to make sure that Kevin's safely back and tucked up in his beddy-byes. But after that . . .

Clara   It's beddy-byes time for you, as well, young man. It's well past your beddy-byes time already. And you know who's paying a visit to you tonight, don't you?

Alexander   Santa Claus, mummy. *(He has managed to gain possession again of Detective Constable Grummett's gun)* Down the chimney. Ker*boom!* Ker*pow!* Ker*poo!* Right in the whiskers! Ker*splatt!*

Clara   Bless his little heart!

Allardyce   Come along then, ladies. The Headmasters' Christmas Eve Fancy Dress Ball beckons to us all!

They go off.

Scene Five

As Scene One, the prison cell. Convicts Gilbert, Crosby and Grummett are spending Christmas Day in prison.

Gilbert   *(singing)* Good King Wenceslas knocked a bobby senseless, right in the middle of Marks and Spencers —

Grummett   Shut up!

Crosby   What's up, Convict Grummett? He isn't hurting you, is he?

Gilbert   While shepherds watched their turnip tops,
             A-boiling in the pot.
             The Angel of the Lord came down,
             And scoffed the blinking lot.

Grummett   I'll spifflicate you, if you don't keep quiet, Gilbert.

Crosby   Some people never change, do they? Leave him alone, Grummett—it is supposed to be Christmas. Goodwill to all and that.

The Warders enter, carrying trays.

Mullins   Here we are, my fine felons. Christmas dinner, such as it is. For growing convicts.

MacBain   A mingy bit of stringy chicken each, some lumpy spuds, some clammy sprouts, and some greasy gravy. Who blew that raspberry?

Gilbert   I don't think I'll bother, thanks very much.

Crosby   Nor me. They didn't say anything about Christmas crackers, did they, in the kitchen? I mean, they aren't dishing them out later on?

Mullins   Christmas crackers? Where do you think you are, Convict Crosby? The Dorchester Hotel? Crackers? In prison! You'll be wanting a date and a mandarin orange next.

MacBain   You're the one that's crackers, Crosby! Well, do you
           want this scoff or don't you?

                    Gilbert and Crosby shake their heads.

           It's a shame to see it go to waste.

Grummett   I'm having mine, I know that.

Warder   I'm not one to say 'no', not if there's a Christmas dinner
           going begging.

                    *The two Warders and Convict Grummett sit
                    down at the table.*

Mullins   It doesn't look too bad at all, that—A bit on the greasy
           side perhaps . . .

MacBain   And maybe a bit cold and clammy, but I've seen worse.
           Them cooks will go spare if all that isn't eaten up . . .

Grummett   Bags I two helpings of Christmas pud.

                    *But before they can tuck in, the horrible hairy
                    spider descends from above and hovers over the
                    Christmas dinner. The Warders and Grummett
                    leap to their feet. With cries of "Help! Help!"
                    and "Save us! Save us!" the three of them back
                    up against the wall of the cell. Crosby and
                    Gilbert snatch at opportunity and duck out
                    through the open cell door, slamming it shut
                    behind them.*

Gilbert   Well, Cros, we've done it again!

Crosby	We have that, Gilbert. Free once more. Where shall we head for this time?
Gilbert	Anywhere, Cros, old lad. But let's keep out of trouble this time, eh?
Crosby	Oh, without a doubt. I've definitely learned my lesson. I'm going to be as good as gold from now on.
Gilbert	No more wanting to chop down Chrissy trees?
Crosby	Not likely. And no more heaving bricks through toy-shop windows. I'm a reformed character—as the saying goes.
Gilbert	And me. Merry Christmas Crozzo!
Crosby	Merry Christmas to you too, Gilly, my old son.
Gilbert	Come on. Let's run.
Gilbert } Crosby }	Cheerio, kids! So long! See you all about somewhere!

And Convicts Gilbert and Crosby seek their freedom.

CURTAIN